Contents

D0530633

Preface

*'Afoot, light-hearted, I take to the open
road, the long brown path before me leading
wherever I choose'*

Walt Whitman

It's a Saturday afternoon in October in San Sebastian, and I'm weaving my way through the weekend traffic, carrying an egg-whisk and a plastic Parmesan cheese container. It's pretty warm and I'm starting to sweat. I'm running faster than I need to because I'm excited. I'm excited because I have the feeling that Richard Nerurkar is going to win the World Cup marathon the next day (as he does). The plastic carton contains high-carbohydrate powder, for making up his drinks with the help of the egg-whisk in my other hand.

I can recall that moment clearly, because I was feeling so happy. I can almost feel the warmth of the sun that day as I ran down the blue line painted on the road. I was happy in anticipation of the race, happy to be alive and running ... and happy to be reaching the culmination of weeks of planning and training.

Twelve hours later, in the cool of the early morning, Richard, my wife Sue and I were jogging along the riverside part of the course. The leaves on the tree-lined street hardly stirred and the water was unruffled. Everything was suspended. The mood was serious, as every runner withdrew into himself before the battle.

Then to the race itself. In the quiet moments before the start we could not know whether that evening would see us celebrating victory or licking our wounds. Within a couple of hours, all was to change. It really was like a battle, with the overpowering throb of the choppers, the screams of the crowd, the pounding of thousands of feet and, at the front, the man-to-man combat of some of the world's finest athletes. This was the experience of running at the highest level, thundering up and down the keyboard of human emotion like a Tchaikovsky symphony, involving the brain, the legs, the guts and the emotions. Whatever the result, we were living.

Of course, I'm lucky enough to be coaching one of the world's best distance runners, but the emotions are no different from those I experienced when my son broke the school record or when I was part of the Portsmouth team which won its first National Cross-Country title. The terror and the elation are the same when I watch one of my athletes line up for a big race as when I first ran for Britain against Russia in the Lenin Stadium.

That was in 1959. Now it's 1995. The body may age, but the mind does not. We are not forced to accept the roles which society allocates us. Experience shows us our mistakes, but it also shows us our successes.

RUNNING IS EASY

If you enjoy something – let's say running – and it does you good, makes you feel better and gives you a sense of purpose, then do it!

It may not be dignified, but it's fun. Every time we stand on the start line, we are making a statement about our belief in ourselves and our potential. Whether you are a good runner or just an average one, the excitement and the challenge are still there and the experience, good or bad, is yours, not something second-hand picked up from a television screen.

The pleasure of running over the downs, along the beach and through the forest is something which I hope will never leave me, but there is more to it than that. It is not just the running, but what you think about when you are running – the sense of purpose which should underlie your running, so that you wake up every morning looking forward to it.

Running is only a part of our lives, and at different times it will become more or less important. There will be times when running, competing and improving are really exciting ... and times when the other roles you have to play in life become the dominant ones. Then you run just because you are a runner, because it is part of your essential nature, something which defines you as a person. Later on, like the leitmotif in a symphony, the theme of your own running will re-emerge and become the melody again.

If I can share with you and perhaps enhance the pleasure which comes from running, something will have been achieved.

Bruce Tulloh
Marlborough, Wiltshire

Why run?

Running is child's play

You don't have to be taught to run. If you watch children in a playground, they run easily. Their style is excellent. They do not all run in exactly the same way, because they have different physiques, but they run in the way which is most efficient for them. Children do not all run fast. Some have natural sprinting speed and some do not. Some have more stamina than others, but at the age of seven all can run.

If you watch these children playing, you will see them chasing each other about, jumping, wrestling and climbing on things. These are the natural human activities. They run about because they enjoy it and when they are tired they stop. When a child is really tired from a hard day's play, he will just sleep until he has recovered. This, too, is natural. The child is simply listening to his body.

Exercise should not be drudgery. It should be something which is exciting and challenging, something which has a purpose to it. We may have to give ourselves artificial goals and rewards, but the closer we can get to that primitive state, the better our bodies will perform.

Running is natural

Man is born to run. We evolved as hunting animals on the African plains, and as the

story of that evolution is pieced together the change of gait is as noticeable as the increase in brain size. In those far-off days, if you couldn't run your chances of survival were pretty slim. The brain and the hands have made us successful, but we still need the legs, the heart and the lungs. In the hundred generations that separate us from our hunting ancestors, little has changed in the genetic sense. Inside commuters' clothing, swarms of nomadic hunter-gatherers move in and out of London every day, but civilisation has tied them down. No wonder they are restless when they gather at the watering holes in the evening; they lack the exercise for which their bodies were designed.

Man in his natural state would alternate between days of hunting and days of feasting, but the nature of his world ensured that it would soon be necessary to get on the move again. Since the invention of the supermarket and the refrigerator, the hunting has stopped and the feasting has become all too easy. Even among children, muscles have become weaker and cholesterol levels higher. The fact that we have to wear shoes affects the way our feet develop. The richer we are in material things, the further away we are from that natural state, and the more difficult it is to get back to the habit of exercise which our bodies need. What was easy and natural to the seven-year-old becomes much less easy

Running is natural – it's child's play!

to the twenty-seven-year-old and may be almost impossible to the forty-seven-year-old. We run to preserve our youth.

Running is good for your health

Back in the Sixties there was a lot of controversy about the effects of smoking on health. Statistics were produced showing that heavy smokers had a much higher rate of lung cancer deaths than non-smokers. Those with a vested interest in the sale of cigarettes countered by saying that there was no actual proof that smoking was the cause of the cancer. They promoted stories about famous people who smoked heavily and lived to a great age and they said that

statistics could be used to prove anything. It was proved that the tars found in cigarette smoke caused cancer in mice, but the smoking lobby said that men were not mice. Rabbits were put onto heavy smoking routines (and became addicted to it) and a high proportion of them developed lung cancer. A link was established between smoking (in humans) and heart disease. The evidence built up, from different sources, until it was generally accepted that smoking was bad for the health.

When the 'jogging boom' started, or at least when it was recognised by the success of Jim Fixx's book in 1977, there was an immediate backlash. There were plenty of people who disliked taking exercise and could find reasons for not doing so, and some of them were doctors. Articles were written with headlines such as 'Jogging Can KILL You', listing all sorts of ailments which might overtake the unwise jogger. However, the evidence continued to build up and we have now reached the point in the 'running and health' controversy where the vast majority of medical opinion and most of the general public are agreed that at least 'exercise is good for you'.

This is an important point gained. It does not really matter a great deal whether people understand precisely *why* it is good for you, as long as they accept the principle and act on it. Without producing all the supporting evidence, I will merely summarise the benefits.

● **Keeps your weight down.** I will go into this more fully in the section on diet, but the equation is simple enough. If you take in more food than you burn up as fuel, you put on weight. If you burn up more food in a day than you take in, you will lose weight. Running itself only uses up about 100 calories per mile, but if you are covering twenty miles a week without increasing your food intake, you will burn up the equivalent of a pound of fat. This is because the running heats you up and stimulates your metabolism, so that you are burning up fuel faster even after you have stopped running.

Of course, if you go out for a long run on a hot day, you can lose three pounds in an hour or less, but that doesn't count because most of the weight loss is sweat, which is replaced by drinking after the run. Weight loss by dehydration is only for fools and for jockeys trying to make the weight.

● **Reduces stress and relieves depression.** Though at the highest level of competition it is very stressful, just going for a run is the simplest way of getting rid of your troubles and making you feel better. The rhythm of easy running calms the nerves better than any spoken mantra, and the pleasant glow which you feel after a run and a shower is more relaxing than any drink. It can lift your spirits, too – one study on depressed patients showed that those who ran improved and remained in better health than those who had therapy but did not run. We don't know whether it is the exercise or just the time out in the fresh air – but it works.

● **Lowers your cholesterol level.** It is known that the reason women suffer less from high blood pressure and its concomitant complaints is that they have more of a certain type of blood protein (Low Density Lipo-Protein) and less of the other type (High Density Lipo-Protein) which is associated with cholesterol build-up. Studies on runners, comparing them with non-runners of similar background, have shown that runners have more of the low-density lipo-protein.

● **Reduces the risk of developing high blood pressure.** This, of course, follows from the fact that their levels of cholesterol are lower, and so the build-up of 'sludge' in the arteries, which narrows them, does not occur.

● **Reduces the risk of strokes and heart attacks.** This follows naturally from the previous statement, and is backed up by evidence from long term studies, over twenty years and more, which correlate causes of death and exercise levels. It is not what you did in the past which counts, but what you have been doing in the last year, and in studies carried out on both sides of the Atlantic on Harvard graduates and on British civil servants, it was found that those who took regular vigorous exercise came out best. Any continuous cardiovascular exercise will do, but, of these, running is the most accessible.

● **Helps you to live longer.** This one is hard to prove, because even if you avoid the degenerative diseases – heart attacks, diabetes, failing kidneys – which exercise protects you from, you have only a certain length of time to live. No one is immortal. Living beings are programmed to die. If there were no death there would be no evolution. What we can say is that regular exercise improves the odds in your favour and gives you the best chance of reaching your full genetic potential.

Running improves your quality of life

A friend of mine gave me for Christmas a wadge of note-pads, bearing the motto 'Jogging doesn't make you live longer – it just *seems* longer'. I would agree with this; to me, life seems full of possibilities. Most people, when they reach sixty, are cutting down on their options; they are ruling out certain things which they are 'too old for'. They are having to cut down on their food and choose the quieter routes through life. This may be sensible but it is not essential. I don't want to sound smug, but as I approach sixty I feel that life is still expanding. I'm planning a training camp in Kenya for the coming winter. I'm making plans for my young athletes who will be reaching their peak at the Olympics of 2004 and I'm expecting to be travelling with them and running with them right through to that time and beyond. The important thing is that you wake up to the new day with energy and enthusiasm and that you end the day with a feeling of satisfaction. Running

helps you to do this. It gives you an appetite for life.

Running makes you look better

You should be happy with the body you are given, and you should make the best of that body. When you are young, your body can handle anything – staying up late, getting exhausted, getting drunk – and still look good, but unless you look after it, it will lose its powers of revitalisation.

Muscles get flabby, fat builds up in places where you don't want it and your skin doesn't glow the way it did when you were seventeen. Running isn't going to make you immortal, but it will give you a good muscle tone and keep a spring in your step. Remember: If you don't want to lose it, use it!

Running is cheap and accessible

As long as you follow the guidelines, anyone can run, and you can start right away without spending any money (except that I would like you to buy this book – but even then you could get your library to buy it). Any park, football field or a quiet stretch of road will do, and you don't need twenty-one more players and a referee. You are not charged for court time and you don't have to pay an entry fee unless you want to run a race.

The start of a schools' cross-country. Remember that each child develops at its own rate.

New York marathons, apart from travelling to races in Wales or Scotland, seeing places they never knew existed and, above all, meeting people in all these places.

Running is a family affair

Unlike most other sports, you can bring your parents or your children, or all of them, to your local Fun Run and everyone can take part. Because it is a non-contact sport, it is safe for the oldest and the youngest.

Running helps you to go places and meet people

If you have been stuck in the rut of shopping on Saturdays and watching TV on Sundays, you will be surprised how getting into running can change your life. It may start with just going to the next town and meeting some different people, and then taking your daughter to the regional championships and then going somewhere with a club team. Your horizons open up. Our local town club, which started with a handful of people in the late Eighties, now goes regularly to the London, Paris and

Running will help your other sports

If you are a weekend sportsman or sportswoman, you don't need to be told about the benefits of exercise, but you will find that regular running during the week will make a tremendous difference to your performance. The more demanding your sport, the more your game will benefit. This applies to games such as football (all forms), hockey (both kinds), lacrosse, tennis, squash and volleyball, as well as to pastimes such as hill walking or board sailing.

Running versus swimming

Running may be only one of many sports, but it is a basic ingredient of most of them. The world of watersports is the exception, and for many people this is a more useful form of exercise than running about on land. Because the water supports your body weight, swimming is a very good form of exercise for anyone who suffers from joint problems. It is excellent for development of the upper body and great for the heart-lung system.

There is no doubt that swimming is very good exercise and a combination of running and swimming during childhood does produce a good all-round physique. This book is written for those who would rather run than swim, but in some of the schedules you will find that swimming is incorporated as part of the training.

Are you fit to run?

If I had a group of fourteen-year-olds who wanted to run, I would not bother with a medical check-up. I would enquire whether any of them had been ill recently, whether there were any asthmatics or diabetics and whether any of them had had trouble with their knees or ankles. If the answer was 'no' to all of these, I would just start straight in with some easy running, allowing plenty of rest breaks for the sake of those who were less fit.

With adults one has to be more careful, but the basic principle is simple. You must walk before you can run. The older you are when you start, the more careful you have to be. It doesn't matter how low your starting level is, as long as you keep on improving.

Do I need a check-up? If you come into any of the following categories, you should have a medical check-up before starting to run:

● Those who have been seriously ill in the previous twelve months.
● Those who have any family history of heart disease.
● Those who are seriously overweight.

It's never too late. Suppose you have had a serious accident or have been ill for many months. You have been confined to your room, you have put on weight, and in any case you have not taken any serious exercise since you left school. You probably think that you are the last person to be thinking about running, but in fact you are the very person who most needs to improve his fitness. This doesn't mean that you have to jump up and start running; it means that you should be making a decision to do something about your condition. The medical idea of health is merely the absence of disease.

You must walk before you can run. If you have done no running or regular sport in the last six months, or if you have had any serious illness, I strongly recommend a walking programme to start you off. The First Steps Programme in the next chapter is quite easy for a young person, but if it looks difficult to you, give yourself two weeks of regular walking before you start. Get into the habit of walking for fifteen to twenty minutes, at least four times a week, and then increase this to thirty minutes, at least three times a week. This will give you time to sort out comfortable shoes before you start running.

Running is the best way of seeing the country.

Should I lose weight first? If you think you have a weight problem, I suggest that you combine mild dieting with the walking programme for at least two weeks, maybe four. Weighing yourself regularly, at the same time each day and on the same set of scales, will show you your progress. Cut down your food intake by no more than 500 calories a day, preferably by reducing the amount of fat, alcohol and sugar you take in, but don't starve yourself – you need energy for your exercise.

First steps

'The longest journey begins with a single step'

Ancient Chinese Proverb

The first step is in the mind. If you are reading these words you have probably already made it – the decision to have a go.

How not to start

Put on any old pair of shoes, get straight out of the door and belt down the road like Forrest Gump until you feel exhausted. Get your breath back and go on running hard until you get home. The next day, do the same again but go further.

If you are young and energetic, and have been taking part in regular sport since you left school, you might just get away with this approach, but for most people it will lead to sore feet, a stiff back, aching calf muscles and a general feeling of exhaustion before a week is out.

Follow life's basic rule: 'If in doubt, read the instructions.'

Getting ready to run

The human foot has evolved over millions of years to become the best possible foot. The wearing of shoes is a compromise we have been forced to make, but running without shoes is still the most natural way

to run, and the method which will do your foot the most good. If you have a nice stretch of grass available, or a sandy beach where the tide has gone out, or a rubberised running track, take your shoes off and try walking and then jogging a few steps. Doesn't it feel easy?

Few of us can walk straight out of the house in bare feet, though, so most of your running is going to be done in shoes. Although our feet are designed to run, they were not designed to run on tarmac, and the shoes will provide the support which you need to absorb the shock of impact.

You don't need specialised running shoes for your first steps, but there are basic requirements for any shoe used for running:

1. The shoe must not be heavily worn down, otherwise you will be thrown off balance.
2. The shoe must not fit so tightly that you cannot spread out your toes.
3. The shoe must be laced up or held on so that it does not flap about when you try to run.
4. The heel should not be more than 1 inch (2.5 cm) off the ground. The flatter the heel, the better.

If you own a pair of trainers, tennis shoes, aerobics shoes or even basketball boots, you can get started. Most types of walking

Fun runners. This is the best way to start – when you're young and full of the joys of life.

shoe will be alright too, as long as they are not too heavy and do not have high heels.

You do not need specialised running clothing, either, to start running. Anything will do as long as it is not too tight, too heavy or too warm. Jeans are okay, but they can be a bit heavy and are often too tight to allow for free movement. Lightweight trousers, T-shirt and sweat top are ideal.

The best places for your first steps, if you are a bit shy, are either places which are so quiet that no one can see you, or so busy that no one will notice you. In a public park, there are lots of people walking the dog or hurrying to work, as well as the regular joggers, so an extra person will not be noticed. If you want somewhere secluded, school playing fields and cricket grounds are usually empty in the mornings, and no one will bother you if you keep to the perimeters.

Are you going to go it alone, or do you need a running companion? This depends on the kind of person you are, but it is easier to keep up your resolution if someone else is a witness to it. Moreover, if you have someone to talk to, it will take your mind off the running. Because running is a natural activity, you can do it without thinking.

Week 1

Goal:	To run at least three times this week.

Day 1.	You've made up your mind, you've chosen a place to start, and you have some suitable clothing. The time of day doesn't matter, except that you should not run on a full stomach. If you have not run since you left school, five minutes will seem quite long enough. Walk briskly for 100 yards, then break into a gentle jog, so that your feet are only just leaving the ground. Keep this

going for thirty seconds, or a hundred yards if you have no watch, then walk for another hundred yards, or until you get your breath back. When you are ready, jog for another thirty seconds. In your five minutes, you will therefore have four of five bursts of easy jogging. Even if you feel that you could do a lot more, please don't. There is plenty of time. If you find that running comes easily to you, you will be able to move quickly through the steps, and in a few weeks will be fit enough to run for miles, but it is vital that you get things right in the first few weeks.

Day 2. No running today. Just walk for half an hour in trainers or walking shoes. How do your calves and ankles feel? In the very first stages you have got to be careful. If you have any twinges, don't move onto the third day until they have disappeared, just keep walking a little each day until you feel ready to run again.

Day 3. Ten minutes of the same walk–jog–walk routine. Restrict yourself to the thirty seconds jog, even if you feel you could do more.

Day 4. Just walking again. I know that I'm being ultra-cautious, but this is far better than rushing into too much running and picking up a strain in your first week.

Day 5. Another 10 min session. This time you can increase the distance of the jogging stretches, if you feel like it. Try doing 200 yards, or sixty seconds. A good way to motivate yourself is to pick out trees or lamp-posts and jog for, say, three lamp-posts before walking again.

Keeping records

This may strike you as a bit pretentious, but it is an important part of reinforcing your determination to become a runner. You can either make a note of it in your daily diary, or you can make out a running calendar and record your progress on that. The first week's programme, if you followed my plan to the letter, would look like this:

Week 1

Day	Planned	Achieved*
1	5 min walk-jog	
2	30 min walk	
3	10 min walk-jog	
4	30 min walk	
5	10 min walk-jog	
6	10 min walk, 10 min walk-jog, 10 min walk	
7	Rest or walk	

*Tick off this column, or write in what you did.

It is important to keep a training log so you can monitor your progress.

Day 6. Walk for 10 min, then, if you feel good, do 10 min of the walk–jog–walk routine, and finish with a further 10 min of walking. You will have covered about 2 miles.

Day 7. God rested on the seventh day and so should you. You have done some running on four days out of the seven, and this is plenty. If you feel any kind of strain in the feet, ankles, calves or knees, give yourself a day's rest or a day of just walking, until you feel ready for the next step. It doesn't matter at all if you take two weeks to get through the first week's programme, as long as you are moving up without injury.

Week 2

Goal: THREE or FOUR days a week of walk-jog, THREE or FOUR days of walking only. The week should include the following, but it does not matter in what order you do the exercises. It is preferable, but not essential, to alternate the harder days with the walking days. If you feel that you are not yet ready to increase the amount, just repeat Week 1 before going on to Week 2.

Day 1. 5 min walk, 10 min of 60 sec jog, 60 sec walk, with 5 min walking at the end.

Day 2. 1 min walk, then 10 min of 60 sec jog, 30 sec walk. If you find this too tiring, revert to a 60 sec recovery after each jog.

Day 3. Repeat Day 1 or 1 hr walking

Day 4. 5 min walk, then 2 min jog, 2 min walk, repeated twice (i.e. three sets in all).

Once you have completed the programme of the first two weeks – even if you took three weeks over it – you have reached a significant point. You have shown that you have both the physical ability and the mental commitment to get into a regular running programme – and from here on, you have no limits. It is time to get properly equipped.

Shoes

Go to a specialist sports shop and get yourself some decent trainers. This does not mean the most expensive kind, just ones which fit comfortably (not tightly) and which give you enough support without being too heavy or lifting your heel miles off the ground. I don't recommend running a long way in tennis shoes, because they don't give you enough support.

The very light shoes are the fastest for racing in, but they do not give enough support for regular road running. You will not need these unless you get serious about road racing. The shoes should fit comfortably when you are wearing a pair of medium-thick sports socks. They will stretch slightly with wear, but if you put them through the washer and dryer they will shrink again. There are few bad shoes on the market nowadays – it is just too competitive – but there are shoes which are over-elaborate and over-priced and are mostly sold to fashion victims rather than actual runners.

Clothing

The old trousers, T-shirt and sweat-top will do fine for training in, but once you are running regularly, and particularly when you are running in warm weather, you will need a change. Now is the time to get yourself some running shorts, if it is summer, or some running tights if it is cold. Personally, I prefer the 'trackster' type of running bottoms. You will also need a shower-proof, lightweight anorak or running top, preferably with a hood. This has the advantage of being wind-proof, and the combination of T-shirt and anorak is a good one, because if you wear a T-shirt, sweat-top and anorak you may get too hot after the first five minutes of exercise.

Commitment

As I said in Chapter 1, you need to fit the running programme into your life rather than just try to tack it on as an extra. In the first couple of weeks it is a novelty and you may be prepared to push other things to one side, but if you intend to keep it going it must become a fixed point in your day. If you can join a running club or just arrange to run with one or two friends at a regular time, then you have a commitment to others, which is much easier to maintain than a merely personal resolution.

Week 3

Goal:	To run at least THREE times in the week, and to run for 5 min non-stop.
Day 1.	2 min walk, then six times (60 sec jog, 30 sec walk), with a few minutes of walking to cool down at the end.
Day 2.	5 min walk, then four times (2 min jog, 1 min walk), plus a cool-down walk.
Day 3.	Repeat Day 1 or 30 min fast walking.
Day 4.	5 min walk, 1 min jog, 1 min walk, 5 min jog, 3 min walk, 2 min jog, 3 min walk.

Week 4

Goal:	To jog for 40 min during the week. We are still not worrying about the speed – that comes later – but just building up the endurance, both mental and physical, without pushing your body so hard that it reacts against the exercise.
Day 1.	5 min walk, then 4-6 times (2 min jog, 1 min walk), plus a cool-down walk.
Day 2.	5 min walk, 5 min jog, 3 min walk, 3 min jog, 2 min walk, 2 min jog, 1 min walk, 1 min jog, 3 min walk.
Day 3.	Repeat Day 1 or 30 min fast walk (or one hour easy walk)
Day 4.	5 min walk, 5 min jog, 3 min walk, 5 min jog, 5 min walk.

If you failed to achieve the forty minutes, or found it hard work, repeat this week before moving on.

You have now reached a point where you can cope with twenty-five to thirty minutes on your feet, partly walking and partly jogging. Where you go from here depends on what you want to get out of it, but I will assume that most of those who are reading this simply want to get fit, stay fit and possibly prove that they are fit by taking part in a fun run or a local road race. If it is your ambition to run the London Marathon, keep reading, because later chapters will take you to that goal.

Distance

How far do you have to run to show that you are fit? If you can jog a mile without stopping, you are fitter than half the population, but if you can't jog for two miles you would probably not consider yourself very fit. I am going to analyse and try to calibrate fitness in the next chapter, but for the time being, let us set a goal of being able to run for twenty to thirty minutes four times a week. This is the kind of fitness that will put you in command of your own body. It will enable you to cope with physical and mental strain far more easily, because it will strengthen your heart as well as your leg, stomach and back muscles. If you can run for as much as half an hour a day regularly, you are certainly fit enough to take part in a 10 km race without disgracing yourself, and at a pinch you could probably manage a half-marathon. On any scale, you could call yourself a runner.

Speed

Human beings are not equal in ability. Indeed, it is our diversity which makes us so interesting and so versatile. The speed at which you can run depends on your body type as well as your fitness. My friend Kevin is tremendously fit. He can carry a forty-pound pack over the mountains for eight hours a day. Swimming a mile is as easy for him as running ten miles – some days he does both – but he will never be a fast runner, because of his build. He has a large, strong upper body, a long trunk and short thick legs. Super-fitness for him is being able to run a sub-five minute mile, and this is only achieved by weeks of hard training. The speed at which you can run a mile, or 10 km, depends on your age, sex, and body type as much as it does on your state of fitness. All that we can do is to try to realise our physical potential. For this reason, the schedules will not tell you to run so many miles in so many minutes. Five miles in half an hour would be an easy run for an elite male runner, a hard workout for a club runner and a total impossibility for most people.

Speed does give you a way of judging your fitness, if you need that kind of reassurance. The relaxed, serene kind of person, who runs just to feel good and stay fit, will not need times and distances, but if you are a compulsive goal-oriented achiever like me you will want to measure your progress and judge yourself against some standard. Hence, you will find some time trials along the way, as signposts to fitness.

Running on the beach – a great place for running

Effort

This is more significant than speed. The body responds to increased effort by getting stronger. If you increase the effort a little bit and give your body time to make the adjustment, you will find that the same speed seems easier the next time. If you increase the effort too quickly and don't give your body time to adjust to it, you merely find yourself getting more and more tired. The programme is set out in weeks, and if at the end of one week you are not ready to start the next, you are pushing yourself too hard. The answer is to repeat the week, with a slightly lower effort level, or give yourself one or two more easy days before moving on.

Week 5

Goal:	To run FOUR times in the week and to jog for 50 min during the week
Day 1.	4-6 times (2 min jog, 1 min walk) Try to jog a little faster than in Week 4.
Day 2.	Pick out a 2-mile circuit. Try jogging the whole of the outward mile, then walk until recovered. On the way back, jog for stretches of 1-2 min, walking for as long as you need to recover.
Day 3.	An endurance session. Jog for 3 x 3 min, walking for as long as necessary between each, then on the way back put in four jogs of 2 min each, with short walks to recover.
Day 4.	Your first timed run. Use either a running track (four laps) or a measured mile on the road. Warm up with 10 min of walking and jogging beforehand, then run continuously for the whole mile and record your time. Walk for 5 min afterwards to cool down.

Week 6

Goal:	To run 8 miles in the week (this excludes walking).
Day 1.	30 min of exercise, made up of three 6 min jogs, with 2 min walking between, plus an extra

few minutes walk for warming up and cooling down.

Day 2. A speeding-up session. Run easily for 3 min, walk for 1 min, then run a bit faster for 2 min, walk until recovered, and run faster still for 1 min. After a recovery, repeat the whole set.

Day 3. Cover the same course as Day 1, trying to jog for most of the way, but walking where you need it. Keep the pace slow.

Day 4. Pick out a course of roughly 2 miles or 15 min of running time. After warming up, try to run the whole course non-stop. Time yourself if you like.

Week 7

Goal: To run 10 miles in the week, and to increase endurance

Day 1. As Day 3 of last week.

Day 2. 5 min of walking or very slow jogging, then six 1 min fast and 2 min slow jogs or walks.You should be running appreciably faster than jogging pace, picking your knees up more and increasing your stride length. It should feel good!

Day 3. Pick out a 4-mile course. Aim to jog slowly over as much of the route as possible, walking only when necessary to get your breath back. Do not time yourself.

Day 4. Three 3 min jogs, 1 min walk, then four 2 min jogs, 1 min walk

Week 8

Goal: Increasing speed.

Day 1. 5 min slow jogging and walking to warm-up, then eight 1 min fast and 2 min slow jogs, plus 5 min cool-down.

Day 2. 30 min of jogging and walking, as for Week 6.

Day 3. 5 min warm-up, then five 2 min runs and 2 min walks, trying to stride out during each run.

Day 4. Timed run over 1 mile, as for Week 5.

Where next?

I know a young woman called Trudie Thomson who started running after her third child was born, when she was already over thirty years of age. Trudie soon discovered that she had a talent for running long distances – not much speed, but unlimited endurance. She moved up to marathons, then ultra-marathons, and within five years of starting she had represented Britain in the World Championships marathon and finished second in the World 100 km championships. Very few of us go that far, or would wish to do so, but it shows you that anything is possible.

If you have been able to move straight through the eight weeks without having to repeat any of the weekly programmes, then

The Hundred Steps

This is both a means of self-assessment and a challenge. I used it in my first fitness book, *Naturally Fit* (Arthur Barker Ltd, 1976). Please note that these steps are not meant to be for successive training days! They measure a gradual increase in fitness and stamina. Everyone should be able to manage Step One, but only a well-trained athlete will be able to reach Step 100.

Step	Distance (miles)	Time (mins)	Step	Distance (miles)	Time (mins)	Step	Distance (miles)	Time (mins)
1	walk 1	20	35	trot 5	50	69	run 6	38
2	walk 1	18	36	trot 3	23	70	run 7	48
3	walk 1	15	37	trot 2	15	71	run 3	18
4	walk 2	40	38	trot 3	22	72	run 7	47
5	walk 2	35	39	trot 4	35	73	run 7	46
6	walk-trot 1	12	40	trot 4	33	74	run 6	37
7	walk 2	30	41	run 2	14	75	run 10	75
8	walk-trot 1	10	42	run 4	31	76	run 7	45
9	walk 3	45	43	trot 5	45	77	run 7	44
10	walk-trot 1½	18	44	run 3	21	78	run 8	54
11	walk-trot 1½	16	45	run 4	30	79	run 8	53
12	walk 4	60	46	run 4	29	80	run 4	24
13	trot-walk 1½	15	47	run 5	40	81	run 8	52
14	trot 1½	14	48	run 4	28	82	run 8	51
15	walk-trot 4	55	49	run 5	38	83	run 5	30
16	trot-walk 2	22	50	run 3	20	84	run 9	60
17	trot-walk 2	20	51	run 5	36	85	run 10	70
18	walk-trot 4	509	52	run 5	35	86	run 9	59
19	trot 2	19	53	trot 6	45	87	run 8	50
20	trot 1½	13	54	run 4	27	88	run 9	58
21	trot-walk 4	45	55	run 5	34	89	run 6	36
22	trot 1½	12	56	run 3	19	90	run 9	57
23	trot 3	32	57	run 4	26	91	run 10	65
24	trot 2	18	58	run 5	33	92	run 9	56
25	walk-trot 5	60	59	run 6	44	93	run 9½	60
26	trot 2	17	60	run 6	43	94	run 8	48
27	trot 2	16	61	run 6	42	95	run 9	55
28	trot 3	30	62	run 4	25	96	run 5	29
29	trot-walk 4	42	63	run 6	41	97	run 9	54
30	trot 2½	20	64	run 6	40	98	run 6	35
31	trot 3	27	65	run 5	32	99	run 9	53
32	trot 3	25	66	trot 8	60	100	run 10	60
33	trot 4	39	67	run 6	39			
34	trot 3	24	68	run 7	49			

Running in the mountains. The fit runner can cope with anything.

you have done extremely well. If at any stage you feel that you are not ready to increase the amount you are doing, just stay at the level you have reached until it feels comfortable – this may well take four weeks, until the body has adjusted itself.

You also have to take account of the other demands on your energy. If other aspects of your life are becoming particularly stressful, don't try to increase the training at the same time, just stay with an amount you can handle.

When you have completed Week 8, I suggest that you repeat the last two weeks, substituting slow jogging for the walking routines. You should now be able to run for 30 min a day, and you have got used to changing pace and running some sections faster. You are probably covering between 3 and 4 miles in your half-hour, totalling around 15 miles a week. You are already much fitter than the average person and you can remain on that level just by repeating Weeks 6, 7 and 8, but not walking at all. On the fourth week of each month I suggest that you have two easy days, jogging for no more than 20 min, and on one day go out for a long run, lasting for 1 hour , in which you will cover 6 to 8 miles. This is a measure of the endurance you have gained – and it should

be enjoyable, particularly if you have company.

The Basic Fitness Programme

This is one level higher than you have reached with the First Steps Programme. It is based on running about 20 miles (32 km) per week, in four sessions. If you reach this level you are doing all the exercise you need to keep you healthy and keep your weight constant. You will also be fit enough to run in the occasional fun run or local race at anything up to 10 km. Anything beyond that is for serious runners only.

The four weeks are all slightly different – one should always look for variety and interest in one's running – but they may be taken in any order. The fourth week is the programme you would follow if you were going to run in a race at the end of it. If you don't run races, I suggest that you give yourself some sort of challenge, perhaps a timed run or a longer run. This gives a little more purpose to the training and enables you to compare your fitness at different times of the year.

Week 1

Day 1.	Steady-paced 30-min run, untimed.
Day 2.	5 min jog, then six 1 min fast and 1 min slow jogs, then six 30 sec fast and 1 min slow jogs home.
Day 3.	5 min jog, then 15-20 min brisk pace.
Day 4.	Long, easy run for 40 min.

Week 2

Day 1.	30 min steady run.
Day 2.	Warm-up, then a 'pyramid' of 1 min fast and 1 min slow, 2 min fast and 2 min slow, 3 min fast and 2 min slow, then 3, 2 ,1 again.
Day 3.	30 min easy.

Day 4.	Hill running, either 30 min on hilly course, with bursts on hills, or running fast up a hill and jogging down again for 15-20 min.

Week 3

Day 1.	30 min steady run.
Day 2.	Fast run round 4-5 mile course.
Day 3.	20 min jog.
Day 4.	Warm-up, then three 1 mile or five 1 km runs, timed, with 3-4 min rest between each fast run.

Week 4

Day 1.	Warm-up, then TEN 400m fast and a 200m recovery jog.
Day 2.	30 min relaxed run.
Day 3.	Rest or 20 min jog.
Day 4.	Race or timed run over 3-4 miles.

If you want to go further, read Chapters 3 and 4 and proceed to the Club Runner's Programme in Chapter 7.

Relaxed running, off the road, should form a large part of your early training.

What is fitness?

You don't need to read this chapter before starting to run. You can go straight in to the 'First Steps' and come back to this when you feel that you need to know more about it.

Fitness is a relative term, not an absolute. It really means 'suitability'. What most people mean when they ask 'Are you fit?' is 'Do you feel alright?' or 'Are you able to cope with life?' So the club football player who can cope with his weekly game, or the serious beer drinker who can cope with walking to the pub and playing a game of darts, or the dustbin man who can swing rubbish bags over his shoulder for six hours a day will all answer: 'Yes, pretty fit'. None of them could cope with a 10 mile run, but then the long-distance runner couldn't cope with heaving rubbish bags about all day and probably couldn't tolerate the bashing of ninety minutes of club football.

You must first decide WHAT you want to be fit for, and then HOW MUCH TIME you can afford to spend on it. A professional athlete could easily spend six hours a day on fitness training, but do *you* need this kind of fitness?

What we are all agreed on is that fitness depends on your heart and your weight – it is a cardiovascular condition. If you get out of breath walking up a flight of stairs that you once used to run up, you know that you are unfit. If you can't get into the trousers you

wore when you were twenty-two, you are overweight. It is in these areas where running gives you the most direct benefits.

To me, fitness means having the capacity to cope with anything life can throw up and still have something in reserve. Can you cope with a full day's work and travelling *and* jog three miles when your car has broken down? Have you the strength to change a wheel on the car when you have a puncture and the flexibility to climb over the back fence when you have locked yourself out?

Do you wake up in the morning feeling strong and positive about the challenges ahead of you? Even more importantly, have you the fitness and the energy to enjoy your leisure time and get the best out of your sport?

Fitness, for an athlete, means something more specific, but even then it is related to the demands of the event. For a sprinter, fitness means being able to run at top speed without pulling a muscle, as well as having the stamina to go through four or five races in a couple of days. Fitness for a middle-distance runner means being able to maintain a fast pace for two or three laps and still have something left for the final sprint. Fitness for a long-distance runner means being able to run hard for ten miles and be fresh enough to run well again the next day.

The mechanics of running

If we take a mechanical view of the body, propulsion comes from the feet, the motors are in the muscles, the bones and joints make up the transmission system, and the fuel is oxygen supplied by the blood, with the fuel pump being the heart.

The transmission system. The running action involves many different muscles. To push yourself forwards you straighten your leg, pushing hard against the ground. The other leg is being flexed and pulled through to the front. At the same time,

Haile Gebresilasie (Ethiopia), world record-holder and world champion at 10,000 metres.

other muscles are being used to keep your body balanced on one leg. Your arm and shoulder muscles are being used to keep the body from rolling from side to side and your back and stomach muscles are being used to keep you upright. All these muscles must have the strength to do the job and the endurance to keep working for long periods.

The beauty of the human body is its adaptability. The leg can at one moment become a rigid pillar which can support a four hundred pound weight and in the next it can become a coiled, flexible spring. This combination of strength and flexibility is conferred by the joints, which can rotate in different planes. The degree of movement in the joint is controlled by the shape of the bones, by the ligaments which bind the bones together and by the elasticity of the muscles.

If there is a weakness in any of the muscles, or in the tendons connecting them to the bones, or in the ligaments which hold the skeleton together, you will find yourself running unevenly. If too much of a load is suddenly thrown onto one muscle, some of its fibres may break under the strain and you have a 'muscle pull'.

If some of your ligaments have stiffened up, whether through age or just through lack of use, you will have less flexibility. This tends to reduce the length of your stride and will slow you down. Because the inflexible runner is more injury-prone, being flexible is part of being fit.

The motors. The muscles themselves will be better at moving you along if they are larger and stronger, so sprinters are usually well-muscled – but for those running longer distances, strength is not the only consideration. The bigger the muscle, the faster it will use up fuel and oxygen. The sprinter uses up fuel so quickly that he does not need any oxygen during the ten seconds that it takes him to run 100m. He is burning fuel without oxygen, by *anaerobic* respiration. Lactic acid* is the by-product of anaerobic respiration; as it accumulates it eventually causes the muscles to seize up – which is why we cannot sprint at maximum speed for more than thirty seconds. After the race the sprinter needs to take in extra oxygen to get rid of the lactic acid. The amount of extra oxygen he needs is known as the *oxygen debt.*

If you are running a mile as fast as you can, you are burning up fuel rapidly and taking in as much oxygen as possible. Your speed is such that some of the fuel has to be burned up anaerobically, so your oxygen debt accumulates throughout the race. This is an event which depends partly on sheer speed and partly on ability to take in oxygen. We can say, therefore, that middle-distance events are partly *aerobic* (with oxygen) and partly *anaerobic* (without oxygen).

If you are running three miles (5000m), most of the energy used up comes from aerobic respiration. The ability to sprint,

*Physiologists often talk about *blood lactate*, or simply *lactate*. The lactic acid splits up into a hydrogen ion and a lactate ion. For training purposes, all these words refer to the same thing.

Hill running – the best for leg strength.

however, is still important, because the last lap of the race is often run very fast. It is mainly (87%) an aerobic event, with a small (13%) anaerobic element. A 10km race is 97% aerobic, and longer races can be regarded as 100% aerobic. The longer the race, the more important is your capacity to take in oxygen.

The oxygen intake system. This consists of the chest, the lungs, the heart, the blood vessels, the blood itself and the enzymes in the muscles. If any one of these parts is less efficient than it should be, it will slow down the whole oxygen intake process. Curiously enough, the size of the chest does not have much to do with fitness. I have measured the lung capacity of dozens of pupils at school and found no connection between the lung capacity and the fitness of the boy or girl. Where you do find a difference, though, is in comparing smokers with non-smokers. With smokers, the little air passages in the lungs are slightly inflamed, so the air cannot travel as quickly. Non-smokers can exhale much more quickly than the smokers, so when it comes to running any distance longer than a quarter of a mile (400m) the smokers suffer. They cannot move the air in and out of their lungs quickly enough to provide the oxygen they need. Smokers are in a similar position to someone suffering from asthma. Fortunately, simply giving up smoking will allow the inflammation to subside and the lung efficiency to return to normal.

Having strong chest muscles does help. I have noticed that children who come into running after having spent some years as swimmers have well-developed chest muscles and are often a year or more ahead in running performance. Many long-distance runners, both men and women, have small, thin upper bodies. This helps in that they have less weight to carry, but sometimes their chest muscles are simply not strong enough to pump air in and out quickly. I always encourage my younger athletes, from sixteen onwards, to use weights in the gym twice a week during the winter. A balanced programme of weight training, which includes exercises for legs, back muscles, abdomen and the upper body will help to correct weaknesses and produce a stronger all-round athlete. A description of weight training exercises is given in Appendix B.

The heart and the pulse rate. Those who become good distance runners are usually born with strong hearts. This is hard to prove because they are not identified as runners until eleven years old or more, but if one compares schoolchildren before they get into regular training one finds that the good runners usually, but not always, have lower resting pulse rates than the average.

You should get into the habit of taking your pulse rate when you first wake up in the morning. It can be found quite easily either by putting two fingers on your neck, a little distance away from your windpipe, or by putting the fingers on the underside of your wrist, in line with the ball of the thumb.

The so-called 'normal' pulse rate is 72 beats per minute for men and 80 beats per minute for women, but this is just an average. It is quite normal for men to vary between 60 and 80 and for women to vary between 68 and 88. Your pulse rate will be at its lowest in the morning. It is slightly higher when standing, compared to sitting or lying, and as you become more active and need more oxygen, your heart rate speeds up, keeping pace. When I woke up the other morning my pulse rate was 52 beats per minute. As I sit typing this book, it is 60. If I get up and walk to the front door and back, it goes up to 64. When I go for an easy run it is ticking over in the 120-130 range, but if I'm trying to keep up with Richard Nerurkar on one of his easy runs it is up to 150 or more. When I am doing a hard session of hill training it might get to 170, which is now my maximum.

The heart is made of muscle and, like any muscle, it responds to exercise by getting stronger. As your heart gets stronger, through training, your resting pulse rate will fall. A world-class athlete can have a pulse rate as low as 30 beats per minute at rest and his maximum working capacity will be when his heart is beating at 180 a minute – six times the resting rate. Moreover, because the heart muscle is flexible, the amount of blood pumped at each beat can go up by fifty per cent of the resting volume. As a result, the athlete working at full blast can pump blood around the body at nine times the normal rate.

This is not the full story, however. We do need to make our hearts stronger, but this is no good unless it can be fully loaded with oxygen as it passes through the lungs. If you are anaemic, your blood is lacking in red cells, which are the actual carriers of oxygen. Someone who was 10% below the normal level of red cells would not notice any difference in normal life, but he would not be able to perform to his maximum as a runner. If your red cell count is higher then normal you will be able to carry more oxygen per minute and be able to keep up a faster speed. This is why runners go to high altitude to train, because where the air is thinner the body makes more red cells to compensate (see Chapter 13).

Having got the blood fully loaded with oxygen, it has got to get to where it is

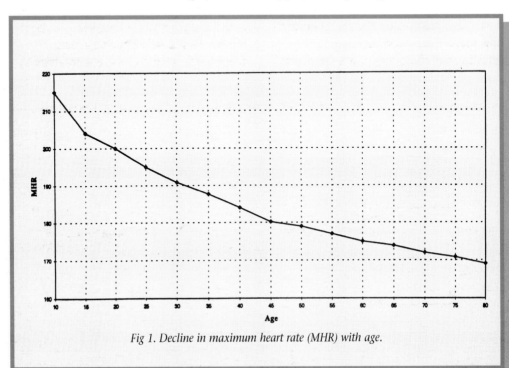

Fig 1. Decline in maximum heart rate (MHR) with age.

needed, in the muscle fibres. There is no problem getting it through the heart and along the arteries, as long as the runner has not got clogged arteries, but deep down in the muscle there is a big difference between the trained and the untrained athlete. The blood reaches the muscle cells in the capillaries, tiny vessels just about the width of a red blood cell with very thin walls. The trained athlete has far more blood capillaries per cubic centimetre of muscle than the untrained person. Thus, even if two athletes had the same body weight and the same body proportions, even the same resting pulse rate, the trained one would be able to perform at a higher level because more oxygen can get to his muscles per minute. This development of capillaries happens slowly, and it is encouraged by running at slow speeds, well below maximum. Sprinting and lifting heavy weights actually

have the opposite effect, because they encourage enlargement of the muscle fibres, leaving less room for capillary growth.

The fuel system. We all have considerable stores of fat. Even a very fit man with less than ten per cent body fat will have ten pounds of fat, enough for many days survival or perhaps a couple of hundred miles of walking. Nature has given man this supply to see him through the hard times, and it has given woman even more, often fifteen to twenty per cent of body weight. Fat contains far more energy per gram than carbohydrate – 39 kilojoules per gram, as opposed to 17 kJ/g – but it requires far more oxygen to produce energy from it. Thus, although we are using our fat stores when going for a very long walk, we do not use this fat when running fast. The energy our muscles use is obtained by

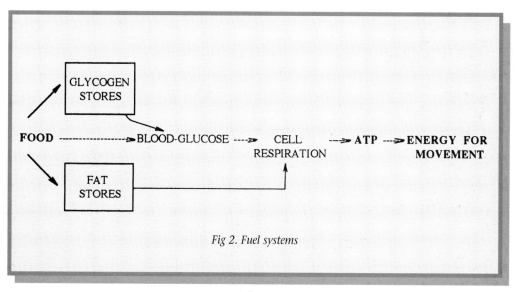

Fig 2. Fuel systems

A case of hitting the wall

After the 1994 London Marathon I had a letter from a runner who thanked me for providing the schedule he used in his preparation. He achieved his target, but unfortunately could remember nothing of the last mile. He collapsed at 25 miles, was put back on his feet, pointed in the right direction, and remembers nothing more until he woke up in the medical tent with his medal around his neck! He was running on empty. This is an extreme example of 'hitting the wall'. The usual sensation is 'dead legs' which simply will not run fast enough, accompanied by extreme tiredness and mental lethargy. For ways to avoid this, see the marathon section in Chapter 13.

the conversion of adenosine triphosphate (ATP) to adenosine diphosphate, with the release of a phosphate ion. Millions of these reactions are going on in our muscle cells all the time, but the supply of ATP is very limited – only enough to keep us going for a few seconds. It has to be regenerated constantly, and this is done by the breakdown of substances deriving from simple sugars. Proteins and fats can also be broken down and thrown into the boiler, so to speak, but the preferred fuel is glucose. This is carried in the blood at a regular but low percentage of 0.1%. If there is the slightest sign of the blood sugar level starting to fall, alarm bells are rung and the body breaks down some of its glycogen stores, converting glycogen to glucose. Of course, we can take in glucose directly through the mouth, but the process of eating, digestion and absorption is too slow for the runner's purposes. Eating food after the race or the training session is fine, because the food as it is absorbed goes to replenish the glycogen.

The glycogen is stored partly in the liver (about 100g) and partly in the muscles (about 600g). This provides enough glucose to synthesize enough ATP to keep us running fast for up to two hours. After this we have problems, as every marathon runner knows who has 'hit the wall'. The brain cells *must* have glucose. They are very fussy and will consume nothing else, so when your blood glucose level drops you start getting hallucinations.

When we are walking or running slowly, a portion of our energy is coming from fatty acids. These are produced by the breakdown of fat. If we have enough fatty acid enzymes in our muscle cells we can use the fats as fuel and thus save some of the diminishing supply of glycogen; this is why pace judgement is so important in a marathon. Those who run slowly all the way never hit the wall, because they are relying more on their fat stores.

It has been discovered that the really fast marathon runners – the 2 hour 10 min guys – do not use fatty acids at all. They are either naturally endowed with enough glycogen or they have developed training and racing techniques to supplement their glucose supply – see Chapter 14.

Inside the muscles. The muscles we use for movement (skeletal muscles) come in three types:

Slow twitch fibres. These have plenty of endurance, contract slowly and respire mainly aerobically. They are found in long-distance runners and in the wing muscles of long-distance birds, like the pigeon.

Fast twitch 'glycolytic' fibres. These contract fast, relying on anaerobic respiration, and tire quickly. They are found in sprinters and in short-distance birds like the chicken.

Fast twitch oxidative fibres. These respire mainly aerobically, like the slow twitch fibres, but they contract quite fast and tire quite quickly. However, they are useful to have for a sprint at the end of a race. There is some evidence that endurance training will convert the fast twitch glycolytic type to the fast twitch oxidative type, whereas speed training will have the opposite effect.

Two runners may be of the same height and weight, yet one is a sprinter because he has predominantly 'fast twitch' fibres and the other is a long-distance runner because he has mainly 'slow twitch' fibres.

You cannot do very much to alter the proportion of fast and slow twitch fibres in your muscles. If nature has given you less than 80% slow twitch fibres, you will never be the world's greatest marathon runner. Sebastian Coe has, I believe, about equal proportions of fast and slow twitch fibres, so that makes him a middle-distance runner, but this does not mean that all those with 50:50 muscle types will be world-class runners.

How can you find out your muscle type? The only true way is to have a muscle biopsy done, which involves taking out a little slice of muscle – rather painful – but experience alone will tell you whether you are an out-and-out sprinter, a long-distance man, or something in between. The muscle fibres carry out energy release, using either aerobic respiration (usually) or anaerobic (occasionally).

When an athlete trains regularly, the muscles respond by increasing the number of mitochondria – the little bodies in cells where respiration goes on – and the amounts of enzyme molecules involved in respiration. Since the respiration process is cyclical, a shortage of only one of a dozen crucial enzymes could slow down the respiration rate and hence affect his running. This is the reason, I suspect, that an athlete often trains well for some weeks or even months before seeing an improvement in his performance. We have not yet reached the stage where we can take a blood sample and see exactly which enzymes are below normal, though we are not far off. In the meantime, all the athlete can do is cover all the options by training at a variety of different speeds, to stimulate the manufacture of every possible enzyme.

What the training does

Continuous, steady running, sometimes known as LSD (Long Slow Distance) will improve the general endurance of all the muscles, as well as the capillary development. After the first few weeks it will do nothing for muscle power or for flexibility, nor for changes inside the muscles.

Running fast, but not sprinting, for any time from thirty seconds to thirty minutes will lead to improved delivery capacity of your heart and blood vessels. When you are running, say, 2000 metres at a pace which is faster than your anaerobic threshold, this is definitely an oxygen intake session. When you are just above your threshold you are accumulating lactic acid; so although you are stimulating the production of the enzymes which break down lactic acid and you are using all your aerobic enzymes at the maximum rate, there will be a point where you have to stop. If you are training right on your threshold pace, which is slower than your 10km pace and equivalent to your 10 mile pace, you are getting excellent training for your heart and for capillary development.

Hill running will develop muscle power in the legs, as well as lactic acid tolerance. Running up long hills, taking two or three minutes over the run, benefits almost all the systems, but what has been discovered recently is that in order to stimulate the production of aerobic enzymes to the maximum, you need to run well above your anaerobic threshold – at a speed equivalent to your flat-out mile speed. The best way of doing this is with bursts of 50-200 metres, repeated many times, with just enough of an interval to recover. This is what I call a 'zapping' session, and we often use it just before races.

To improve the supply of fatty acids, which will help the marathon runner, the best thing is long slow runs on an empty stomach. This should encourage the manufacture of the enzymes which consume fatty acids, but it may make the runner slower at 10,000 metres. The top-class marathon runner would do better to find ways of increasing his carbohydrate supplies.

Causing damage

When you run really hard, muscle cells start to leak. The production of lactic acid without enough recovery time for its levels be brought down damages the membranes. The pounding of the feet on hard roads damages muscle cells and blood cells, and the reaction to this is stiffness, caused by excess fluid. If the athlete tries to run hard with stiff muscles, muscle fibres may get torn and stick to other fibres, causing pain. Training for too great a distance lowers the amount of stored fuel in the muscles so that cells cannot repair themselves. In extreme cases of over-training the white blood cells, which form a vital part of the immune system, may not be manufactured in sufficient quantities to do their job, making the athlete more susceptible to infections.

If we give the body the right amount of stress, it strengthens itself in order to deal with that stress; but if we give it too much, it starts to break down and recovery may take a long time. The secret of successful training is to give the body just enough stress and not too much.

Summary

Total fitness for the long-distance runner means that he must maximize his potential in the following areas:

1. Low body weight, with a low body fat to encourage heat dispersion.
2. Very well developed leg muscles with a good capillary blood system and a high proportion of slow twitch fibres.
3. A large strong heart to pump the blood around the body.
4. Strong and flexible chest muscles for taking in air rapidly.
5. Strong but flexible joints in the ankles, knees and hips.
6. Strong muscles in the abdomen, back and upper body to keep the right posture when running hard.
7. Muscular endurance at racing speeds.
8. The right mental approach – resolute, ambitious, yet adaptable and resilient.

How to train properly

Most of us start by copying someone else's training, or by following a schedule from a magazine. Assuming that you have selected a schedule which roughly approximates to your present fitness level, this is better than nothing, but you will be a very lucky person if it suits you exactly. After a bit of trial and error you will find out how much running you can take without becoming over-tired. You are now ready to construct your own progressive schedule.

The basic principle of training is that you train until you are tired, rest until you are recovered and then train again, but that little bit harder. You have to remember that the recovery period is as important as the training period. After making an effort, the body adjusts – muscle fibres grow, fat is broken down, more enzymes are manufactured – but if the effort is too great or the rest period is not long enough the body never gets a chance to strengthen itself. If it has not had the chance to finish clearing away the debris from the previous blitz before the next one comes along, the result is that the runner feels more and more tired and stiff. In serious cases of over-training the immune system is damaged, because blood proteins are broken down. This results in the athlete

being more liable to infections, so that both your general health and your running performance suffer. Very often, more is lost through the illness than is gained through the extra bit of hard training. The very things which make runners what they are – ambition, determination, irrepressibility – very often lead them to overtrain, to keep on going when they should stop.

The wrong way to train

My friend Helen took up running this year. She is a good swimmer, so was already used to exercise. Once she got used to running three or four miles a day, she started to time each run. For a couple of weeks her times got better as she learned to push herself harder, but after that the improvement tailed off and the time came when, however hard she tried, she was running outside her records most of the time. She started to get depressed about her running. Why was she no longer improving in spite of trying hard?

You will understand the reason if you understand the pattern of effort and recovery which the body needs. By making a hard effort every day, she was just becoming more tired. Because she was running

Richard Nerurkar in training with coach Bruce Tulloh in San Sebastian.

Designing a training programme

You have to start from where you are. If you have been running ten miles a week, it would be crazy to embark on Richard Nerurkar's 120 miles-a-week schedule. The first thing you must do is assess your state of fitness and the amount of training that you think you can handle for the first few weeks.

It is not just the running, but also what you think about when you are running.

the same distance every day, she was not improving her endurance and because she was running the same speed every day, she was not improving her speed. Perhaps most importantly, because she was doing the same kind of training over the same courses day after day, she was not getting the stimulation which comes from variety of pace and venue. Once she stopped timing herself every day, and was content to put in more relaxed and slow running between the hard efforts, she started to enjoy it again, and so she continues to improve.

One of the best training axioms is: 'When in doubt, ease off.'

Always remember that there is plenty of time. One day of missed training can easily be made up in the following week, whereas the effects of one day's over-training, or one race too many, may last for several weeks.

Self-assessment

Let us assume that you have been running seriously for a year and have taken part in some 2½ -mile fun runs, a five-mile race and a couple of 10km races. Bear in mind that fun run courses are not as a rule measured accurately – at best someone may have driven once round in a car. Let us say that your best times were:

2½ miles (4 km)	17 min
5 miles (8 km)	42 min
10 km (6.25 miles)	49 min

Work out your average speeds in minutes per kilometre or minutes per mile, remembering that a tenth of a minute is six seconds. We get the following results:

Distance	Average speed
4km	4 min 15sec/km
8km	5 min 15sec/km
10km	4 min 54 sec/km

Assuming that the distances were correct, this suggests that you are at the moment better over the shorter than the longer distances. Of course, one is bound to slow down as the distance gets longer, but the expected difference between one's speed over five or six miles (8-10km) compared to three miles (5km) would only be about 10-15 sec per mile (6-10 sec per km) The fact that your speed over the 5 miles was slower than that for the longer 10km race could be explained in all sorts of ways. Perhaps the weather was cooler when you ran the 10km

race, perhaps the course was flatter, or you were just in better condition. Even allowing for inaccurate courses, we can say that your present state of fitness allows you to run faster than 4 min 30 sec per kilometre over distances of 3 miles (5km) or less and at speeds of below 5 min per kilometre for distances of 10km or less. This gives us an idea of the sort of pace to train at in the interval and repetition sessions.

Now take a look at the kind of running you have been doing in the past year:

● For how many weeks in the year have you been doing what you regard as 'good training'?
● How many times a week were you running?
● How many miles or kilometres a week were you covering in those good weeks?
● What was the average distance you were running in a single day?
● What was the distance of your longest run?

Before we set new training goals, you must also look at your health and fitness during that time:

● How often were you ill? (include colds and coughs)
● Did you have any injuries which arose from your running?
● Can you trace the cause of the injury? (see Chapter 12)
● Did you have any times when you were 'fed up' with running or when your performances declined for no apparent reason?

If you have kept records of your training and performances in the past year, you will now be able to say: 'On *this* amount of training I was going well and feeling good, but on *this* amount I was either doing too much training or doing the wrong thing.' Even if you haven't got everything written down, at least you will have some idea of how much you were able to take.

If you are a complete beginner, you will be starting on the First Steps Programme. At the end of this you are up to fifteen miles a week, running four or five times a week and averaging about four miles on each run. Your longest run may be six miles. If you have followed the programme carefully, repeating a week whenever it was necessary, you will have suffered no injuries.

Early days

For the first two weeks at least, you should be doing only the amount of running which you know you can handle, but you must try to keep to the routine you have set yourself. Err on the side of caution. The most important thing is to establish the running habit so that it fits in with the rest of your life. If you have decided to do, say, three thirty-minute runs during the week and one forty-five-minute run over the weekend, don't do any more than that. If it is well within your powers, it will be that much easier to move up later on. Make the pace as slow as you like.

What we are doing here is building the endurance base for the better quality training which comes later. The more solid the base, the better it will be able to support the next phase.

If you feel fine after two weeks, increase the volume of the running by either ten per cent or by a maximum of four miles and, without worrying about the quality of the running, do at least two weeks at this increased volume.

Warming up and cooling down

In the early stages all your running should be at a comfortable pace, stopping to walk when you feel you need to. Quite soon, though, we shall come onto running at a faster pace over short distances. Before trying this faster running, you should be properly warmed up. Cold muscles just do not work as well as warm muscles. It is not just a matter of warmth; when you have been through your warm-up routine you will have increased the blood flow to the working muscles, so that they can get the extra oxygen they will need for faster work. You will also have improved the mobility of your joints and the flexibility of all the supporting muscles and ligaments, making you much less liable to get a muscle pull.

The basic warm-up routine is 'Jog-Stretch-Stride-Jog'. When you start, it is better to have too much clothing on rather than too little, then you can discard layers as you get warmer. Start jogging as slowly as you like. If you are running first thing in the morning, you may be just shuffling along with a stride length of about two

Catherine McKiernan and Paula Radcliffe, two of Europe's best, battle it out.

The very minimum should be two laps of the track, 800m, and the longer you have been training hard, the longer should the warm-down be. When you have been running hard, you have generated a lot of heat and much more blood is being diverted to your skin. Your shirt and shorts

feet. This doesn't matter. Jog for at least five minutes, or until you feel that all parts are in working order, then go through the Basic Seven Stretching Exercises (see Appendix A) which will take you another five minutes. Only after that should you start your striding, which means running for fifty yards or so with an increased pace and stride length. After each one, walk or jog slowly until you have got your breath back, then try another fifty yard stride, a little faster. After five or six strides you should have worked up to something close to your maximum sprinting speed.

A pre-race warm-up will be longer than this (see Chapter 13), but after you have finished it is important that you keep warm and loose until you start your faster running. If you just stand around and get cold, your warm-up will have been a waste of time.

After the training is over, you must always finish off with a cooling-down routine. This is an essential part of the training.

may well be damp with sweat. If you suddenly stop running and stand still, the drop in body temperature could be quite serious. The other reason is that there will be fatigue products (mainly lactic acid) and a lot of extra fluid in your leg muscles; as you jog slowly; this will be pushed out of the muscles, so that you will be much less stiff the next day.

Building endurance

Man is designed to run. There is almost no limit to the amount of running which the human body can take, as long as it is given time to adjust. When I was running across America I ran 1000 miles in the last 20 days – that is 350 miles a week– with no ill effects, and I am sure that the limits could be extended much further than that. Given adequate rest, food and massage, 500 miles a week is quite possible.

However, demands on time force us to compromise, and, in any case, merely running a lot of miles is not the way to produce the best performance. I merely mention these distances to put things into perspective. Modern man finds it pretty tough to get out of his car and run a single mile, and running a marathon is regarded as a terrific feat, yet people in the Third World have a completely different outlook. One day, after running in a meeting in Kingston, Jamaica, I set out with some friends to climb a peak in the Blue Mountains. We had to leave in the early hours of the morning to get to the top just after dawn, and as we left our car and started up through the foothills, we met the market women coming down with their baskets. While we young strong athletes regarded the fifteen or twenty-mile round trip as a good day's exercise, these women were covering a similar distance as part of their day's work.

The first thing you have to decide is how much time you are prepared to give. This time then translates itself into miles, depending on your running speed. What I have suggested as the Basic Fitness Programme is four half-hour sessions of running per week, plus whatever weekly sport you enjoy. The total mileage will be 15-20 per week. This level of fitness is really as much as you need if you are running for health and fitness, with no competitive intentions. If you become a regular club runner, your commitment will be of the order of thirty to forty minutes a day on four weekdays, plus an hour on either Saturday or Sunday. This gives you a mileage of 25-35. The more serious runner

will be putting in an hour a day on most days, with one easy day and one long run of an hour-and-a-half – total seven hours a week, probably 50 miles a week or a bit more.

The easy way of doing things is simply to increase your daily running, without increasing the speed, until you have got up to your target in terms of hours per week. This means that your joints and posture muscles get used to the extra strain before you increase the quality of the running. If you have been at the level of the Basic Fitness Programme, the safe way to move up to the Club Runner's Programme, as given in Chapter 8, would be:

Weeks 1–2	18–20 miles (29–32km)
Weeks 3–4	21–23 miles (35 km)
Weeks 5–6	25 miles (41km)

You will be increasing your endurance in three ways – by the number of runs per week, by the distance of your daily run and by the distance of your long weekend run.

Remember that the body takes time to adjust to a heavier training load. I suggest that three months is the minimum amount of time you need to get used to the 15-25 miles (25-40km) a week, and after that you need at least six months to adjust to the Club Runner's Programme. For many people, this level of training, getting up to a maximum of 40 miles (64 km) a week, is quite enough, and you can go on improving for several years, gradually improving your endurance and converting your body into the body of a runner.

Chapter 4

Crash courses

It may be logical to move your training volume up by a few miles every six months or so, but that does not always fit in with your plans. If you suddenly decide that you are going to run the Kathmandu Marathon in three months time, and you have a week's holiday coming up, you can have a training blitz and double your normal mileage, or you can have a weekend training camp with your friends and run six times between Friday and Sunday evening. It's good fun once in a while to break out of the usual patterns – but just remember that after it you need to give yourself a few days to get over your exertions. Don't suddenly jump from thirty to sixty miles a week and think that you can go on at sixty. Better to have the next week back at thirty.

Increasing your oxygen intake

In the first few weeks this will increase just by doing regular running, whatever the speed, but there will come a time when it will not improve without some faster running in training. The increase in what we call 'the aerobic capacity' is the most beneficial and the most important feature of running training, and everyone is capable of improving in this respect. It is this aspect of increasing fitness on which most serious athletes concentrate.

In simple terms, if you want to run faster, you must get used to fast running. This is what we mean by 'quality training' – training which contains a high proportion of fast running.

How fast is 'fast'?

This depends on the individual, and is measured by the pulse rate. If your resting pulse rate is 60 and your maximum pulse rate is 180, the difference between them is 120.

If you are running fast enough to push your pulse up 50% of the way towards maximum, i.e. 120, you will just be starting to get a training effect. The best training effect is gained when your pulse rate is somewhere between two-thirds and four-fifths of the way towards maximum, i.e. between 140 and 156 in this case. Another way of judging it is by your racing speed. Effective training is done when your pulse rate is round about its 'threshold value' or a little higher. This is the point where, if you go any faster, you start to respire anaerobically and build up an oxygen debt. Your threshold rate corresponds roughly to running at your best ten-mile speed, so running at your 10km speed or your 5km speed is good training, because you will be well above the threshold pace. Of course, the faster you are running the less time you can keep going, but by running at a variety of speeds we can improve all the different functions involved in taking up, transporting and using oxygen.

Race distance and training distance

It seems obvious that the longer the distance you are training for, the longer your training should be, but this is not always the case. What happens is that people fit in as much training as they feel they can afford. A club runner training for a marathon may be able to manage a maximum of fifty miles a week, while an international middle-distance runner, who races over 1500 metres, might be doing 100 miles a week in his winter training. To get near your potential at the 10km distance, you must be averaging at least 30 miles (50km) a week, and for a half-marathon at least 40 miles (64km) a week.

There is a rule of thumb which says that it is possible to run three times your normal training distance on a one-off basis.

Thus, if you train five miles a day, you will be able to manage a half-marathon, even if you suffer a lot after it. The implication is that if you are used to running 9-10 miles regularly, you will be able to run a marathon.

The 12.5 rule

This is another rule of thumb, the result of practical experience.

For every increase of 12.5 miles (20km) you will get a ten per cent improvement in your race performance.

It works pretty well at 0-20km, 20-40km and 40-60km, but after that another rule applies – that of diminishing returns. A step-up in weekly mileage from 37.5 miles (60km) to 50 miles (80km) will bring some improvement, but probably no more than five per cent and after that you have to work more and more to get a slight improvement. The upper limit, for all events except the marathon, comes at between 80 and 100miles (130 and 160km) a week, and for many runners 80 miles a week of good training is more beneficial that 100 miles or more of mere plodding.

Running speed

The beginner naturally asks: 'How fast should I be running?' Many beginners anxiously time themselves round the same course day after day and work out their average speed. Experienced runners never do this. They work at a variety of different speeds, some faster than race pace, some at race pace and the majority of miles at slower than race pace. By working at different speeds they put stresses onto all the different areas involved in the running action – lungs, heart, leg muscles and fuel systems. The other benefit of doing this is that the training is much more interesting than just going for a run every day.

The most effective forms of aerobic training are:

- Interval training
- Fartlek
- Repetition running
- Hill and resistance running
- Brisk 'aerobic' runs
- Races and time trials

43

Interval training. This is the most scientific way of doing it, in fact it was first started by a German cardiologist for the rehabilitation of his patients. It proved so successful that he used it as a training method for the middle-distance runner Rudolf Harbig, who proceeded to smash the world record for 800 metres. It was used very effectively by the great Emil Zatopek, who won Olympic gold medals for the 5000 metres, 10,000 metres and marathon at the 1952 Games in Helsinki, and by the Hungarian coach Mihaly Igloi, whose athletes broke a whole clutch of world records in the late fifties. It forms the basis of the training of most if not all of the present international runners.

The schedule is this: You run a fairly short distance fast, and after a short interval for recovery you run fast again. You repeat this for a set number of runs over a fixed distance – say 12 times 400 metres – with a 200 metre recovery jog, in 2 minutes, as the interval.

This is an infinitely flexible system, as one can vary the distance run, the speed of the run, the length of the interval and the number of times the run is repeated. If you run on a track, everything can be precisely recorded, so that the coach and runner can see how one training session compares with another. If we can also measure the athlete's pulse rate at the end of each run, even more useful information can be gained.

The term 'interval training' is usually applied when the distances run are between 200 and 1000 metres. When the distances are longer it becomes 'repetition running'. You might ask why we only run at three-quarters of the maximum heart rate. If we want to improve, why don't we just run as fast as we can each time?

The reason for this is that flat-out running is at least partly anaerobic running, so lactic acid accumulates. This prevents our muscles from working efficiently on the next run, unless we have a very long recovery time. If a club runner set out to run twelve 400 metres on a 'flat out' basis, his times for each 400m with a 2-minute recovery, would look like this:

1st 400m	58 sec
2nd 400m	61 sec
3rd 400m	63 sec
4th 400m	67 sec
5th 400m	69 sec
6th–12th 400m	70–75 sec

If the same runner did a controlled interval session, starting at 67 seconds per lap, he could probably average between 65 and 67 seconds for the whole set and finish up feeling strong and fast, rather than completely shattered. He would recover more quickly the next day and would certainly be able to do another quality session 48 hours later, while the 'flat out' training system would leave him stiff for two or three days.

The attractions of interval training are, firstly, that one is running quite a long distance at a speed faster than one's racing pace. Secondly, the runner and the coach know exactly what has been done and so it

A perfect day's running.

is easy to measure and to see improvement. As well as bringing the physical benefits, it builds confidence and teaches pace judgement.

Fartlek. This is a Swedish word meaning 'speed play'. It embodies the principles of interval training, in that one is running a lot of short repeats at a fast speed, but the distance, the speed and the recovery time are left up to the runner. If you are feeling good you can do fast bursts with short recoveries. If you are still feeling a little tired from the previous session, you just run a little slower or give yourself a longer recovery. The best part about it is that you don't need a running track. Fartlek is best done in nice surroundings, off the road, in a forest or through a park. For the highly motivated athlete this can be as hard a session as interval training, but in general it is less strenuous. A lot of athletes put some structure into it by making the fast bursts and the recoveries last for a certain time or

distance, e.g. ten x 1 minute fast, 2 mins slow. Another way of doing it is by counting strides; if you count each time the right foot hits the ground, you will find that when you are running fast a hundred double strides will take about one minute. A session of 'one hundred fast, one hundred slow', repeated ten times or 'fifty fast, fifty slow', repeated twenty times, will take you about twenty minutes. Again, it is infinitely flexible. A top-class runner might do six x 2 min and six x 1 min and six x 30 sec, with a 60 sec recovery each time. At the end of the session he has run for 39 minutes, which includes 21 minutes of fast running.

Repetition running. This consists of sustained fast runs, usually at 10km pace or faster, with rest periods during which one walks or jogs.

It is tougher than interval training because you are keeping up the fast pace for longer, so it is better training for the oxygen delivery system. In a good repetition session, as with a good interval session, one will cover more than one's racing distance in the fast parts of the session. A serious 5000m runner might do a session of four x 1 mile or six x 4 min, with a 2-3 min recovery. A good session for a 10,000m runner would be six x 1 mile or five x 2000m.

Hill and resistance running. This is very good training for leg strength as well as for aerobic capacity and there are very few good runners who do not use hills at least some time in the year. The Kenyans use hills all through the year in training, and when they come to running on the track or on flat cross-country courses they put 'artificial hills' into the race by changing the pace and running a couple of laps at an increased effort. This usually has a devastating effect on their opponents.

To be effective for aerobic training the hill should take at least thirty seconds to run up, but it can take as long as two or three minutes. If it is too long, one wastes a lot of time running back down to the bottom, but of course one can always do a 'Hill Fartlek' session by running round a hilly course and putting in a burst up each hill. Sebastian Coe and his father who coached him were great believers in the value of hills for winter training. Not only does it toughen you up physically, it is tremendous mental training. Every hill you climb makes you feel that you have achieved something – and so you have! One winter, when I could only train after work and I was living in a small country village, the only way I could do hill training was by putting two cycle lamps on my path up the hill. This meant that I could keep to my training plan even if there was no moon.

In resistance running we are doing the same thing – running with increased effort– but making the extra effort either by running through difficult going, sand, snow or thick grass or by running with extra weight. Running in army boots is one way – Dave Bedford used it on his way to breaking the world 10,000 metres record – and other methods include wearing a weighted vest or running with a motor tyre on a rope behind you. This kind of session should not be done more than once a week, otherwise it tends to distort the normal running action.

Fast 'aerobic' running. All running apart from sprinting is aerobic, but it is only when you get towards your threshold value that you start to stress your oxygen transport system and so start to get a training benefit. Since your threshold speed is the speed that you can run in a ten-mile race, you won't be able to keep this up in all your training runs, but if you are running at your half-marathon pace, which is just below the threshold value, you should be able to keep it up for three or four miles. If you are running at your best marathon pace, you should be able to keep it up for seven, eight or even ten miles, which is long enough for most training runs. You have to bear in mind, too, that you will be wearing heavier shoes, which will slow you down by five to ten seconds per mile.

In terms of pulse rate, if you have a resting pulse of 60 and a maximum of 180, your threshold might be 160. In a 'brisk aerobic' run, your pulse rate will probably be over 150 for most of the run, rising to 160 on the hills and dropping to 140 over the last mile, when you should be easing off.

The advantage of track running is that you can measure exactly what you are doing.

getting better, and it gave me a lot of confidence.

As I mentioned earlier, timing yourself on every run is not a good thing, because you become too time-obsessed. Your times will not go on improving indefinitely. Day-to-day changes are bound to affect your running speed; the most significant one will be how fresh or how tired you are. When you do a time trial, it should be at a carefully chosen time when you are physically rested and mentally prepared.

How hard should you train?

You should not be training at one hundred per cent effort every day. No one does – or, let us say, no successful athlete does. The body needs time to recover from one hard effort before it can get the benefit of the next one. On the other hand, it is not a good thing to train at exactly the same effort level every day, because if you don't increase the effort, you won't improve beyond a certain level. A lot of people go on the 'Hard-Easy-Hard-Easy' routine, which means that you are usually putting in three hard efforts a week, say, Tuesday and Thursday hard, plus a race or a long run at the weekend. You need to ease off before the big efforts, so that your body

In terms of speed, if you can run ten miles (16km) in 60 minutes, then six minute miles is threshold pace. Your marathon speed will probably be 6.30 to 6.40 per mile (about 4 min per km), so your 'brisk aerobic' pace will be between 6.10 and 6.30 per mile (3.45 to 4.00 per km).

Time trials and races. Races get you fit, as long as you give yourself time to recover after them. They also tell you how fit you are. Racing, however, is quite stressful, so you may prefer to get the same benefits by timing yourself over a fixed course on the road at regular intervals. When I was a young and ambitious athlete, I had such a course down at my home in Devon, which I thought was about two miles. Over three years I brought my time down from 9.5 min to 8 min 16 sec, which led me to think that it wasn't two miles, but as I went back to the course every few months and improved my time I knew I was can rebuild its fuel stores, and you need to decrease the intensity of the training after a race or a hard training session, because the body needs to repair damaged cells.

Another commonly used method is to go 'Easy-Moderate-Hard', on a three-day cycle, with the seventh day being either a rest day or a long run, depending on your fitness and your ambitions. This enables you to adjust your training to your state of fitness; as you get fitter, you can get more good training done on the 'moderate' day, which will either be a straight run or a Fartlek session. Eventually, you can reach a point where you are doing four good quality runs and a long slow run in each week.

Fartlek running is best done in the woods.

Training at the right pace

Training is specific. If you are going to race over a mile, you have got to get used to running at that speed, and the same goes for 5000 metres, 10,000 metres, half-marathon and marathon. However, you have also got to develop the various qualities outlined in Chapter 3 – endurance, speed, oxygen intake – and this means doing different sessions at different speeds. All distance runners should include some running at 800 metres (half-mile) speed and some at marathon speed, as well as the speeds in between. It is the balance which is different. The marathon runner will probably only do a few fast strides a week at his 800m speed, and the 800m runner will only do one run a week at marathon speed, but the top-class runner does cover the whole range of pace, and so should the club runner. The training schedules in Chapters 7–11 give examples of this.

Building strength

It is muscle which generates speed. The faster you want to run, the more muscle power you need. Sheer strength and power – the maximum force which your leg muscles can exert – is essential for sprinters. However, distance runners have to compromise. The more time they spend on sprint-based weight training, the more they tend to convert some of their muscle fibres from the aerobic 'slow-twitch' type to the anaerobic 'fast-twitch' type. On the other hand, a slightly-built distance runner, with a weak upper body, will gain by improving his all-round musculature.

As soon as you are basically fit, start some speed training.

in quick succession, with two or three sets of exercises being performed in a training session. The right time to start weight training is in early winter, so that the athlete can get in a three-month training period. As he then moves to serious competition, either indoors or over the country, he will then reduce the volume and the intensity of weight training, maybe switching over to circuit training to maintain all-round strength.

The older runner, too, can benefit from weight training. Over the first two or three years of his training he can improve his strength – after that, the time needed to make much more improvement would be better spent on running, so I would recommend either a short 'refresher course' once a year, or the use of circuit training. See Appendix C for Strength Training Exercises.

Strong legs, which every distance runner needs, can be built up in the weights room or on the hills and sand dunes. It is no coincidence, I feel, that two of the great icons of middle-distance running, Sebastian Coe and Herb Elliott, did a lot of weight training and gym work in their close season. At the other end of the scale, the men who are breaking world long-distance records, such as William Sigei, Kahlid Skah and Yobes Ondieki, do very little weight training, relying on hill work to build up their legs and strengthen their back and stomach muscles.

My recommendation, based on what is practicable, is that from the ages of eighteen to twenty-one young runners *should* be using weight training. They should be doing a circuit of eight to ten different exercises, covering all the main muscle groups, but with an emphasis on leg strength. Because we are looking for endurance as well as strength, the weight will not be so heavy that it cannot be lifted ten to twenty times

Building speed

Making your muscles stronger will not automatically make you run faster. Your body must be flexible enough to give you a good stride length and your muscles must be 'educated' into running with a good sprinting action. Even if your ambition is to run a decent marathon, you can benefit from speed training, because it teaches you how to run smoothly and efficiently.

The top-class distance runner uses many of the training techniques of the sprinters in order to run as efficiently as possible. Have you ever seen a picture of a sprinter or a 400 metres runner in full stride? The knee of the lead leg is coming well above waist level, the arms are driving vigorously backwards and forwards, to prevent the body from twisting and the ankle of the back leg is fully extended. The sprinter uses every leg muscle fully and develops every leg muscle fully, while far too many long-distance runners only use a fraction of their available muscles. Certainly, the distance runner needs to run economically, so he will not run with an enormous stride, but if all the muscles in the leg are making their contribution, the thigh muscles, which provide most of the drive, will not have to work quite as hard.

The way to improve your action is to practice a set of 'sprint drills' twice a week, as part of the warm-up for an interval or repetition session. The most important drills to practice are the four described in Appendix B:

- High Skipping
- High Knees
- Bounding
- Bottom Kicking

Putting your schedule together

You have now decided how much training you can do in a week, and you are aiming at a particular event or series of events – let us say some road races between five miles (8km) and ten miles (16km). In the short term, it is best to plan your training over ten to thirteen weeks, with two or three weeks to get used to the volume, six to eight weeks of progressive training and then two to four weeks of racing.

It is essential to have a sense of progression, rather than the feeling of repetition. I like to work to a two-week cycle, so that the harder timed sessions do not repeat themselves too often. In the build-up part of the training you can try out an interval session, a hill session, a repetition session and a time trial. You don't have to do the full session or keep strictly to the time intervals – just get an idea of what is possible. In your interval training you might be running 400 metres at a time, on a track, with half a lap jog as your recovery. Run the first lap at a 'comfortable' speed and time it. Run the next one a couple of seconds faster and the next one a bit faster still. You will soon find out the speed you can maintain for a set of 10 x 400m.

When you next go to the track, fix your recovery time – say 2 min for your 200 metres jog – and the number of fast runs, say ten. Try to stick to your target time for the first part of the session and then see how it goes. You may be able to speed up or you may have to slow down, but be sure to complete the session and record your average time. This is the benchmark against which you will measure yourself two weeks later.

As you move into the serious phase of your training, start with one hard effort and one long run a week, then progress to

Always wear reflective clothing when running at dawn or dusk.

two hard efforts a week. When you have a race at the weekend, make sure that you have at least two easy days or rest days between the last hard effort and the race. This is the pattern that I have followed in the 'ready-made' schedules at the end of the relevant chapters.

Tapering

This is where the volume and the intensity of the training is tapered off in the pre-race period. When one is racing every week, it is normal to taper by having a reduced session two days before the race and a rest or just an easy jog on the day before. Before a big race, however, it is usual to cut out hard training for four or five days beforehand and for a marathon, where the runner has usually been under a big training load, it is normal to start the tapering with three weeks to go, to reduce the penultimate week considerably – down to half or two-thirds of normal – and then to do nothing but easy runs in the week before the race. Just as intervals are necessary in a training session and easy days are necessary in a week, the tapering before a big race is just as important as the training itself.

Personally, I find that complete rest is less beneficial than a daily jog of thirty minutes, because the runner's body is used to regular exercise and he will not eat or sleep as well when deprived of his daily 'fix', but the main thing is to avoid getting tired. One should have a feeling of gathering strength and a feeling of eagerness to race which overrides that other pre-race feeling of being scared stiff.

Summary

The essentials of a training programme are:

1. Set yourself a target.
2. List your training objectives, e.g. endurance.
3. Divide your training into phases.
4. Within each phase, get variety into your programme.
5. The nearer you get to your race, the more you should be training at around race pace.
6. Give yourself enough rest before and after the big efforts.

Running and lifestyle

Get your priorities right

What are the most important things in your life? Most of us would start by saying 'my family, my friends, my career', and then a little further down the list, in no particular order, '...my house, my possessions, my sport, my hobbies'.

Haven't you forgotten something? Top of the list comes 'Survival'. This is the thing which we fight for when it is threatened, but it is something which is placed so deeply in the subconscious that it need not be spoken. You can see it in a baby, who regards himself as the centre of the world, and in the toddler you can see this instinct being submerged, so that it emerges less and less in childhood.

In the adult the self-preservation instinct is still there, often governing our decisions without us realizing. I would expand this 'survival' instinct to one of 'maintaining our psychic and our physical well-being'. We only realize the importance of this well-being when it is not there. We have a duty to ourselves first of all. Unless we are in good mental and physical condition, we cannot properly fulfil our roles as parents or lovers. The relationship between the individual and his employer is always a difficult one. An employer's instincts tell

him: 'This person belongs to me. He is an extension of my will and should act according to my will, not his own'; whereas the individual's instincts tell him: 'I am my own master. The employer may pay my wages, but he does not own me. All I owe him is an honest day's work.'

Curiously, the flag of individualism which is waved most proudly by Western democracies can become a major constraint on our individual freedom. In place of the big institutions, with their nine-to-five jobs, their sports clubs and their low wages, we have instead the smaller, more aggressive companies which pay more money to fewer people, but demand a one hundred and ten per cent commitment. You are expected to get into the office early and you stay on until the day's work is done, which may be very late. The company is successful and you get paid a lot of money, but your lifestyle suffers.

Young men and women should not be put into a position where the work they do has an adverse effect on their health. If they were working in an atmosphere contaminated with asbestos dust or tobacco smoke, their complaints would receive the maximum support of the law; but if the threat to their health lies in the stress they are under, the pressure to work long hours to show that they have what it takes, there is no redress. And what about the middle-aged employees? The effects of pressure on them are likely to be even more drastic. In the short term it may seem more cost-effective to employ the minimum number of people and work them to their limits, but over the course of years the company is going to be more effective if its employees are treated like human beings and encouraged to pursue a healthy lifestyle.

What I am getting round to is that *the right to play is as important as the right to work*. It is important that you construct your working life so that there is time for physical and mental recreation. If you are an employer, it is important that you recognize that right. The physical element is disappearing from more and more jobs, hence the need increases for physical exercise outside working hours.

If you are a runner you must programme running into your daily life, not just try to stick it on as an extra when time allows. If you are taking up running, you have to make space for it, otherwise it will not last when the flames of enthusiasm die down. If you really care about the kind of life you lead and the way your children are going to grow up, you should put these priorities at the top of the list.

Let's start with the small things. You want to be able to run with your friends after work in the evenings – so make it a fixed arrangement that on certain days you always finish work at a certain time. You would like to go running in the park with your partner during the lunch hour – so

arrange to have a longer lunch break and stay a bit later on those days. You want to run to and from work to get yourself fit – so make sure that your office has somewhere to shower and change. You may well find out that you are not the only person to appreciate this.

Consider the larger decisions, about where you live and work. Earning the highest possible salary is not necessarily the way of giving yourself and your family the best possible life. Would you not be better off living in a smaller town for a smaller salary than working in a city and commuting for three or four hours a day? Have you considered moving to Swindon or to Spain or to South Australia? Being a runner makes you realize that you can make your own decisions about the direction of your life. It may be difficult to keep yourself from being swept along with the mainstream, but if you paddle your own canoe hard enough it can be done.

Running and social life

Running can be selfish and running can be anti-social, but it doesn't have to be. When you are training for the London Marathon and the schedule demands that you do an eighteen-mile run over the weekend, it is bound to clash with something. At the level of the elite runner, it is simple. He puts running first and everything else takes a lower place. Occasionally, the 'normal' runner may be able to exercise such a privilege, but only if he has managed to avoid imposing his running demands on the

R U N N I N G   I S   E A S Y

A training camp run – the best way of getting a lot of training done in a short time.

family throughout the rest of the year. There are several ways of arranging things.

1. Always run early in the morning. This is alright if you are just concerned with getting in two hours of running a week for the sake of your health, but personally I find that I cannot run hard early in the morning, so I use that time for my easy recuperation runs.

2. Put in a short hard session in your lunch hour or immediately after finishing work. This is fine if your workplace has somewhere to change and shower. It does mean that when you get home, you are free to do other things.

3. Do your running on the way to and from work. Of course, you need to live within a few miles of your work. My friend Jerry used to commute by train, change in the train and run to the office from the station. After work he used to change at the office, run to the station and spend the first fifteen minutes of the journey doing his stretching exercises in the train. He had to solve various complications about carrying clothing, changing and showering, and he got some funny looks on the train – but he kept it up.

4. Give yourself a routine where you dedicate, say, two evenings a week to training, and do this immediately after work. This means that you are free after eight o'clock on those days. For the other weekdays you can swap you programme around so that your rest day or days can be fitted in with your social life, and your easy running can be done in the early morning.

5. Your weekend running does not have to be at the same time every time. If you have to visit your grandmother on a Sunday either do your long run between 7.30 and 9.00 am, or get yourself dropped off twelve miles from your destination and run the rest of the way.

6. Marry another runner. Your children will put up with it until they realize that not everyone runs all the time!

Running through the year

One of the things which I hope you will get out of this book is the realization that you are in charge of your life. Just because you have joined a running club and there are races every weekend all the year round, it does not mean that you have to take part in everything. As with crops, there is a lot to be said for 'lying fallow' for part of the year. I once coached a very good Kenyan athlete, Mike Boit, whom I had known when he was a student. He competed successfully at international level for fourteen years, but for three months of the year he never ran a step. He is the type of person who does not put on weight easily, and in three months he could get back to full fitness. More importantly, the break from running prevented the build-up of fatigue from continuous training. He was able to train very hard in the early summer, before the racing season, and race every week through the summer at the highest level, but he never developed any long-term injury problems.

The point here is that you don't have to keep running all the time like a man trying to go up the 'down' escalator. You are free. It doesn't really matter if you have to miss running for two or three weeks because you are moving house. It doesn't matter if you take a month away from running to go round the Greek islands, as long as the running habit has become part of your normal life.

I am glad to say that running *is* addictive, but it is a healthy addiction, because it is a natural attribute of the human condition. The more it becomes a regular activity, the easier it will be to get back into it after a break. Moreover, you will probably find yourself packing a pair of running shorts when you go away on holiday.

Scheduling the year

There are times when it is easy to run, times when it is difficult to run and times when you just don't feel like running. It is up to you to construct a pattern which will ensure that you are still running this time next year and still running in ten or twenty years time.

Running in autumn

This is the easiest time to run, because the weather is fine but not hot, the ground is dry and the scenery at its best. It is the best time to start or to make a fresh start. Children go back to school; the routine of work s re-established; the autumn evenings are still long and Christmas is a long way off. The beginner can work his way through the first few weeks and the more experienced runner can start to builds up his mileage with no pressure of time. The pace does not matter. You can run through newly harvested fields, with the stubble crunching under your feet, or you can run along dry towpaths where the first leaves are beginning to settle.

This is the time, too, to get some friends together to run with you. If you can get into the habit of meeting regularly in the autumn, you are more likely to keep going when it gets dark and cold. It is a good idea to have some event to aim at, such as a local road race, towards the end of October. This will be the first test of your running ability. It is also the time when you find out how much running you can manage comfortably in a week.

Running in winter

For the British, this really means December, January and February. The drawbacks are the dark and the cold, icy roads and increasing pressure around the Christmas and New Year period. Unless you are a committed runner with serious goals, this is the time to keep your running at a minimum. It is better to cut it right down, even if this means running twice a

Running with a friend, off the road, builds up endurance without stress.

week, rather than to drop it completely, because it is always harder to get started again after a break. At two half-hour runs a week you will not lose much fitness. You are continually reminding your body that it is a runner's body, so it keeps itself in readiness. There are a few basic principles which will make running in winter easier and safer (see box).

Running in the spring

In Britain the weather starts to improve in March, but in the USA or Scandinavia you may need to stick to the winter routine until April. This is the time to increase the quality of your running. Spring and autumn are the peak seasons for competitive road racing. If this is your goal, you need to be fit enough to get into one of the programmes in Chapters 7 and 8. This means increasing the amount of running gradually from the winter level. Injuries occur when one makes sudden changes, so increase the amount first and then gradually bring in faster sessions.

Spring is a good time too, for training holidays. It is a good time to go somewhere where it is a little warmer, or even just to get a change of terrain and run in new places, to rekindle the pleasures of running. I like to go down to Devon and run on the beaches and the sandhills. The sand is clean and the beaches are empty. You need to be prepared for cold winds and sudden showers, but it is tremendously invigorating.

The right clothing

The Russians have a saying:

'There is no such thing as bad weather, merely unsuitable clothing.'

They should know. I have managed to keep running through a bad winter in New England; I wouldn't recommend it, but having the right clothing is the secret. The much derided 'shell suit' was designed for running in cold weather and is the ideal garment, because it is light enough not to restrict your running, while providing insulation and protection against wind and rain. The alternative is to wear running tights or tracksters with a sweat top and, if necessary, a lightweight hooded anorak. Woolly hats and gloves are essential winter equipment – in fact, I find that if my head and my hands are warm, I can run in most climates without tights or track-suit bottoms. This means that I can run faster and train more effectively.

It is absolutely necessary to wear reflective clothing. Many shoes and track-suits carry reflective strips, but the reflective mesh vest, which weighs nothing and can be tied over the top of any other clothing is, literally, a vital piece of equipment – because it can save your life. Anyone who drives a car knows how difficult it is to see runners and cyclists on dark roads, if they have no reflective gear.

At this time of year it is much better to run in the middle of the day if you can. If this is impossible, why not maintain your fitness during the week with a couple of exercise sessions in your local sports centre or gym? Aerobics classes, exercise bikes, treadmills and rowing machines all give you good cardiovascular exercise. If none of these are available, use my Winter Maintenance Programme.

Winter Maintenance Programme

Once a week, probably over the weekend, put in a forty-minute run. Start by jogging round a ten-minute loop, wearing plenty of protective clothing if the weather is bad, then discard as many layers as possible and run for at least thirty minutes.

Twice a week, choose a small circuit close to home, approximately a mile or a ten-minute slow jog. Go round this slowly with full protective clothing, come in and stretch for five minutes, then go out and run briskly round the same circuit, finishing off with one more slow lap, wearing your protective gear. This will only take you half an hour in total. It may not be very exciting, but it will be sufficient to keep you basically fit until the weather improves.

Running in summer

This depends on what kind of summer it is. The British climate allows us to train through the summer with very few concessions to the weather, but even here one has to make allowances for heat when competing. Hot weather running in many parts of the world can be very uncomfortable, even dangerous, unless you take the right precautions. Those who are at the most risk are the running fanatics who go off on holiday to a hot climate and do not make

A change of terrain will help you rekindle the pleasures of running.

allowances for the weather. You *can* run in hot climates. I ran as much as fifty miles a day in high temperatures when I was running across the USA without suffering any problems, and I have run, albeit slowly, in high temperatures – up to 42 degrees Celsius – and high humidities, in Queensland. The precautions are merely applied common-sense, but they must be applied.

Sunburn protection. If the sun is really fierce, run in the early morning and just before sunset. If you have to run in the heat of the day, wear a cap and a baggy T-shirt which will allow air to circulate. If you burn easily, apply sun-protection cream to your nose and cheekbones, your arms and the back of your legs. Use common-sense and start with no more than twenty minutes in the sun, increasing the time as you build up a tan.

Drinking water. In hot dry climates you will lose a lot of liquid even when running slowly. It is a good idea to drink a pint (500ml) of water just before you start to run, and to run in loops so that you can get a drink every fifteen or twenty minutes. If you are racing in hot climates, take water at every drinks station, even when you are not feeling thirsty. After training, some people like to take salt tablets with their water. Generally, we get plenty of salt in our diet, but if you are doing really big mileages, say 15 miles (25km) a day or more, then extra salt might be a good idea.

Those who are most at risk are those who rarely expose themselves to sunlight even in cool climates. I recommend running without tights or tracksuit bottoms for most of the year, so that your legs get a natural protective tan as well as your face. If you run in a singlet when the weather warms up, you will get your arms and shoulders tanned too.

Ageing

This is dealt with in Chapter 12.

Alcohol

Personally, I don't object to a beer or two. I enjoy it, it helps me to relax, and I know that my liver will metabolise the alcohol within an hour or so. I know that it is a poison, in that too much alcohol will start to kill cells, and I know that it is potentially addictive, but I have a more powerful addiction – to running, which prevents me from drinking too much. If I do have a lot to drink at a party, I take a large glass of lemon or orange squash before going to bed in order to counteract the dehydration effect.

The truly dedicated athlete does not drink at all – except perhaps a glass of champagne when he has won his gold medal – and I expect that he is right. He is less likely to become addicted to it, so he is less likely to develop the drinker's diseases in later life – obesity, diabetes, cirrhosis of the liver – and in the short term he runs no risk of upsetting his training or racing by having alcohol in his system. However, call me old-fashioned if you like, but I believe that life is to be enjoyed and that 'a little of what you fancy does you good' – as long as you remember that a lot of what you fancy does not do you a lot of good.

Sex

I could remark that having sex during the race definitely loses you time, but that would be too frivolous for a serious book such as this. There is a theory that a sexually frustrated athlete, like an angry athlete, is more aggressive and performs better. It is for this reason that sportsmen are often separated from their wives and girlfriends before big events. There may be individual cases where this works, but the tense, frustrated or angry person is

Water Station in a long distance trail run. Taking on water is essential for survival.

less stable and less predictable – a loose cannon.

I find that athletes perform well when they have a stable background and that includes a normal sex life. For the fit athlete, not a great deal of energy is expended, relaxed people sleep better and , what is more, as Woody Allen said, 'It really clears out your sinuses!'

Sleep

There is an old English saying which goes 'Six hours for a man, seven for a woman, eight for a fool'. When you are training hard, you will probably need at least eight hours in bed, and younger runners need more than this. When we are in training camps, we reckon to have at least an hour's sleep after lunch as well as the eight hours at night. Take as long as you need and don't feel guilty about it.

Runners worry most about sleep the night before a race. It is not the lack of sleep which will affect their race, but worrying about it. As long as your body has its seven or eight hours horizontal, it will have all the energy it needs for the race, in terms of blood sugar and stored glycogen, and the muscles you need will be rested. The adrenaline pumping round your system, which gave you a sleepless night (though probably less sleepless than you imagine), will make you run faster on the day. The person who never gets nervous never performs well. When you are training hard you never have difficulty in sleeping – if you do, it is a sign of over-training. The time when you need

to get enough sleep is in the week leading up to the race, when you are recovering from the hard training you have done before. If you are a busy person, as many runners are, don't keep on doing things right up to bedtime. Give yourself a bedtime routine to make sure you calm down – a bath, a milky drink and some time reading or listening to some good music. Above all, give yourself time to relax.

Running and stress

Paradoxically, running can be both a stressful occupation and a cure for stress. Just as war brings advances in surgery, so the fight against AIDS has both increased our awareness of the importance of the immune system and produced a vast increase in the amount of research done in this area. It is unfortunate, though not surprising, that far more research is done on the sick than on the healthy.

What is it that distinguishes the 'very healthy' from the normal? Athletics coaches are constantly experimenting on their athletes, whether consciously or not, by seeing how much training they can take. Up to a certain level the athlete improves in performance, to a measurable extent, but there eventually comes a point where the training is too much. The athlete becomes more and more tired and eventually breaks down. This breakdown is often seen in the form of listlessness, loss of appetite and poor sleep pattern, accompanied by susceptibility to infections. Conversely, the athlete who has the right training load feels full of energy and is hardly ever ill. To understand the reasons behind this, one must go back to Dr Hans Selye, the Canadian who pioneered the investigation of stress in a holistic way. His book *Stress without Distress* (J B Lippincott, New York, 1974) had a great effect on my approach to training. His concept is simple yet all-embracing – that stress is non-specific. When the body is placed under any kind of stress it alters its hormone balance. Not only adrenaline, but chemicals like testosterone, the human growth hormone, the glucocorticoids and mineralocorticoids show an increased output, while the production of others falls. It doesn't matter what the stress is; it may be the stress of moving house, working for exams, playing too many games of football or simply worrying about something. Up to a certain point stress is beneficial. We perform with greater energy and increased awareness. If the stress increases still further, however, the output of anti-stress hormones will eventually start to fall. This has an effect on the entire metabolism, including the rate at which our cells grow and are repaired and the production of the cells in the immune system.

The concept we have to bear in mind is the Total Stress Load. For the sportsman the formula is:

Lifestyle Stress + Emotional Stress + Training Stress + Competition Stress = Total Stress Load

The fit athlete *should* be better able to withstand stress more than the ordinary person, because he or she is trained to be able to perform well under pressure. However, if the athlete is training too hard or competing too much, a slight increase in the total stress can push them over the top. It is a sad fact that fitness is not the same thing as health; the highly tuned athlete may be less 'healthy' than the club athlete who maintains a high degree of fitness without going over his physical limits.

Being aware of the 'total stress load' concept enables the individual to maintain equilibrium and to avoid succumbing to the effects of over-stress. Remembering that a moderate amount of stress is good for us, we must balance an increase of stress in one area with a decrease in another. The top-class athlete must bear in mind that he needs a stable emotional and economic background if he is going to train and compete at the highest level.

As Ian Stewart recently said about training: 'It is really what I would call commonsense – except it doesn't seem to be very common.'

Lifestyle stress. The sportsman needs an economically stable base. He should not be adding to his stress by worrying about mounting debts. Thus a part-time job which pays enough for basic living but allows time for training is better than a well-paid but demanding job, and better than having no job and a lot of financial worry. The aspects of where you live and how much travelling you have to do must be considered, too. The college-based athlete in America, the state-supported athlete in the old East Germany or the heavily-sponsored athlete in Western Europe have had all this stress removed from their lives. A lot of people think that becoming a full-time athlete would solve all their problems, but too often it causes increased stress and worse performances.

Emotional stress. This is something we can rarely control, but we can adjust other aspects of our lives so as to diminish the total stress load. During times of great stress one should use training as a form of therapy. As Kipling said:

'If you can fill the unforgiving minute
With sixty seconds worth of distance run...'

I would have recommended forty minutes worth, myself. One should avoid serious competition when under great stress – though non-serious competition is fine.

Training stress. Training must be progressive, and very gradually progressive at that. The increase in volume and the introduction of new training methods must all be done gradually, with one phase merging into the next There must be regular pauses to make sure that the body can adapt to the extra load before increasing it further. Each hard session must be followed with recovery time before the next one is attempted. It is a mistake to try to improve quality and quantity at the same time. Train first for the distance, then improve the quality.

Competition stress. Since competition is at the heart of sport, one would never say 'avoid competition', but I would say 'select competition' and the selection must take into account the other stresses in your life. One can train to cope with this kind of stress and the thinking athlete – or the thinking coach – will plan out a competitive series in which the challenge gradually increases. As each challenge is successfully met the athlete's confidence grows, until he is ready for the highest level.

One must realize that going into this level carries with it the strong possibility of failure – something which the up-and-coming young athlete may not have met. Being able to handle failure and come back again is the most valuable lesson that sport can teach you.

Coming back to the more mundane level, one can use the concept of 'total stress load' to control one's day-to-day health and fitness. There are a few simple guidelines.

1. When lifestyle stress or emotional stress increase, competition stress should be avoided, and training should take the form of therapy – hard or easy – according to how you feel.

2. However great the pressures on you, some time should be set aside every day for physical exercise. Thirty minutes a day, five days a week, is the minimum.

3. Even when not taking part in competition you should monitor yourself as though you were an athlete in training. Your eating and sleeping patterns

should be as regular as possible. A daily check on your resting pulse and a weekly check on your weight will tell you if anything is going wrong.

4. It is good to be an athlete when you are thirty, but when you are fifty it is essential.

Smoking

Everyone has had the anti-smoking doctrine preached to them at school. As a biology teacher I have preached it for thirty years. In the short term, smoking causes inflammation in the bronchioles, making breathing more difficult. This will clear up pretty quickly if you stop smoking, but continuous smoking leads to long-term damage and is a major contributor to heart disease and lung cancer. Smoking may be a pleasure, but you are gambling with your most precious possession – lifelong health. In the short term it will not affect sprinters, because they do not rely on aerobic exercise for their performance, but over the course of time it will impair their ability to train properly. You don't see many people smoking at dinner after an athletics Grand Prix meeting. If you are already a smoker, think about the positive aspects of being really fit. The more you concentrate on what you want to do, the less you will need to smoke.

Diet

One big advantage of being a runner is that you can eat a lot without putting on weight. The more you run, the more you can eat. The needs of the average sedentary man can be met by 2500 calories a day, but a runner putting in 10 miles a day can consume at least an extra 1000 calories a day. I say 'at least' because your metabolism is speeded up after running, so that you continue to burn up fuel at a faster rate even at rest.

I do not believe that diet has very much to do with athletic performance. 'You are what you eat' is much less true than 'you are what you do'. The proof of this, to my mind, is that you can take a World Championships field and find amongst it athletes of widely different cultures, with enormous differences in their dietary habits, yet the differences in their performances are measured in fractions of a second.

I don't think that there is anything you can eat which can make you run faster, but I will accept that a diet which is consistently deficient in certain vitamins and minerals will limit your performance. One of the spin-offs of eating a large amount of food is that one is very unlikely to suffer from a deficiency of any of the trace elements. From the point of view of the elite athlete, I'd like to look at the way we tackle certain practical problems.

The regular daily diet. As long as you emphasize variety, you should cover all the necessary vitamins, and the problem may be just one of preparing and eating enough in a day to get the necessary calories. My rules are:

63

Pasta and salad – two of the basics in the athlete's diet.

i)	Each meal should include either fresh fruit or salad, or both.
ii)	Each meal should include a major source of carbohydrates, which can be added to as necessary.
iii)	Water should be taken immediately after each training session, and some food as soon as possible afterwards.

The hard-training athlete may need 4000 calories a day and since more than half those calories should come from carbohydrates, he should be eating over 500g of carbohydrates a day. A large plateful of rice or pasta represents about 4oz (112g) of the food in its dry form, which is mostly carbohydrate. The athlete needs to eat four to five times this amount per day, depending on how big he or she is and how much training is being done.

When we are in a training camp, the daily menu looks like this:

Breakfast:	Fruit juice or fresh mango/ pineapple/pawpaw Porridge with milk and honey Toast and marmalade ad lib A banana, tea or coffee
Lunch:	Soup, with a lot of bread Pasta with a simple sauce Green salad or coleslaw Bread and cheese if needed Fresh fruit
Supper:	Fish, chicken or meat dish, with large amounts of rice, potatoes or pasta and a green vegetable Fruit salad or rice pudding, tea or coffee

In addition to this we often have a cup of tea and some bread or cake right after training. Most runners drink at least half a pint of water or dilute juice immediately after each training session, and when the mileage is really high they drink high-carbohydrate drinks such as High Five or Leppin, where you mix the powder in with the water.

I have made no specific mention of fibre content here, because by eating a lot of fresh fruit and vegetables we get all the fibre we need. The same goes for proteins, because in addition to the protein foods of the main course, there is an appreciable amount of protein in bread, potatoes and pasta.

Diet on your travels. A big problem for the modern sportsman is that he is taken away far too often from his stable environment, where he is probably getting an adequate diet and forced to buy food, often from fast-food outlets at stations and airports. The guidelines here are:

i)	Take a packed meal with you, so that you can get what you want.
ii)	Carry a water bottle with water or dilute juice in it, so that you don't get dehydrated.
iii)	Carry a reserve of fruit and chocolate and/or muesli bars.
iv)	Try to eat a small meal every 3–4 hours, rather than starving for hours and then stuffing yourself when you arrive.

Pre-race meals

This is where it is easy to make mistakes. Athletes, being very nervous, often don't feel like eating, but on the other hand some people eat too close to the competition, then find that their food does not digest as quickly as usual.

You should finish your meal between three hours and five hours before the start time of your race. If you have breakfast at eight and your race is, say one o'clock, that is fine, but if your event is at two-

Fresh fruit and vegetables are needed every day.

thirty I would recommend having a drink and a snack at eleven. Incidentally, you can go on drinking right up to the start of your race, and in hot weather I would recommend this. Use plain water, squash or an isotonic drink, but avoid taking a lot of tea or coffee because of their diuretic effect.

The right things to eat at this stage are those which are easily digested, non-fibrous, with a high carbohydrate content. Fibrous foods can lead to an attack of 'the runs' just before or during the event, which is very unsettling.

Foods recommended: White bread or toast, ripe bananas, honey sandwiches, chocolate bars, cereals such as cornflakes or rice crispies which are low in bran.

Foods to avoid: High-fibre foods such as muesli, fatty foods such as fish and chips, milk shakes, fried bacon and eggs.

A recipe for disaster

I recently went on a training camp with a very promising young British athlete. The way he ran in training was terrific, but his eating habits horrified me. His daily menu when at home was:

Breakfast: Sugar-frosted cornflakes, cup of tea
Lunch: Microwave baked potato, with sauce, crisps, Coke.
Supper: Takeaway burger and chips or fish and chips, Coke.

Additional energy was made up by chocolate bars or more chips. He rarely ate fruit and never ate salad or vegetables. In spite of this he performed extremely well last winter. Does this show that bothering about diet is a waste of time?

I think it shows that in the short term it is inherited ability plus training which matter most, but it is also my opinion that his competitive career will be interrupted by injuries and illnesses if he does not change his diet.

Post-race meals

After a big effort your body is dehydrated and your muscles are low in glycogen. The first need is to replace the fluid, and I would recommend an isotonic drink here, unless you have been running a very long way, in which case a high-carbohydrate drink is best.

If you can put back some of the fuel within the first hour after the exercise, your recovery rate will be much quicker. The enzymes which were used to break down the glycogen are the same ones that bring about the re-synthesis of glycogen, and they are present in high concentrations in the muscle cells immediately after the exercise – so take in some simple carbohydrate food as soon as you can tolerate it.

Special events

If you are running a marathon or taking part in an event which goes on for several hours, your requirements are somewhat different. For a start, because you will be exercising at a slower rate for some of the time it is alright to have some fat in the meal at the beginning of the day – provided you have time to digest it. It is also a good thing to keep on snacking every hour-and-a-half, so that your glycogen stores can be topped up, and it is essential to keep taking fluids. This is where the commercial replacement drinks come into their own and you should choose one which has a balance of water and salts, plus enough carbohydrate to meet your energy needs, but not so much that it upsets your digestion. In a marathon, you should be taking drinks every three miles, and in a long-running sport you should take drinks at least every half-hour if possible.

Carbo-loading

There is definite evidence that you can store up extra glycogen just before a long endurance event, if you take in extra carbohydrate at the right time.

In the last few days before a marathon you will be tapering off your training, running three or four miles a day instead of ten to twenty. Hence you will tend to build up your stores even without eating anything special. If you are competing in a marathon on a Sunday, I recommend that the last bit of effort – a brisk six or eight miles – should come on Tuesday afternoon, and after that the athlete eats only smallish amounts of carbohydrate for the next 48 hours. Excessive depletion is dangerous. From the Thursday evening, for 48 hours, he should take large amounts of carbohydrate – 10g of carbohydrate per kilo of body weight per day and large amounts of water. This will cause him to put on weight. On the Saturday he should have only a normal evening meal, so as not to upset his digestive system, and the following morning he should have a normal breakfast. The extra glycogen stored can make all the difference to the runner's energy reserves – hungry men do not make the best fighters if they are weak from hunger!

Running and other sports

In the last few years we have come to appreciate the value of 'cross-training' – that is to say using training and even competition in one sport to increase fitness for the primary sport. If you have read all of

Chapter 3, you will appreciate that we can divide fitness into different areas:

● Cardiovascular (heart-lung)
● General Endurance
● Local Muscular Endurance
● Strength
● Flexibility
● Speed

Some sports score highly in all areas, others in only a few. Hill walking, for example, scores highly for general endurance and moderately well for heart-lung fitness, but only poorly for most of the other categories. There is also the 'damage factor', which assesses the risk associated with each. A summary of all these factors is given in Table 1 on page 69.

The indoor sportsman

If you work in a city in North America or Northern Europe, you probably spend a couple of hours each day travelling to and from work. You are the kind or person who wants to lead a full life and wants to be fit and healthy enough to do it. The best way of doing this is to join a gym in the city, near your office, where you can exercise whatever the weather, without wasting even more time on travelling, and make this an enjoyable social occasion at the same time.

Joining a health club will not make you fitter any more than buying a diet book will make you slimmer. You need a programme which will give you something to enjoy and something to aim for. I will assume that you are going to be taking part in some sort of race in the spring and the autumn and maybe even a short-course triathlon in the summer. You also want to maintain your muscular strength. The right programme for you would therefore be:

Tuesday and Thursday
30 min in the gym, consisting of:

10 min running on the treadmill
10 min strength work
10 min on the exercise bike or ergometer

Wednesday and Friday
20 min in the pool

Saturday
One hour's cycling or 30 min swimming

Sunday
40-60 min running

The balance would obviously alter during the year. In the eight weeks leading up to your race, you would cut down on the swimming and run four or five times a week instead of three. When the weather outdoors was really bad, you could concentrate on either swimming or weight training for four weeks to build up that aspect of your fitness. Change your programme at least every three months in order to keep yourself interested.

Treadmill running

The motorised treadmill, as found in most gyms and leisure centres, has to be treated as a specialised form of running. I have known people to get injured by switching suddenly to a lot of treadmill running, without breaking themselves in. The running action is slightly different and one needs time to adjust. Remember, too, that running on a treadmill is easier than running on a road, and covering five miles in half an hour, say, on a treadmill, is a good bit easier than doing it on a static surface. Add at least fifteen seconds a mile onto your treadmill performances to get a road equivalent. However, the general principle applies that if your treadmill performances improve, you are getting fitter, which is what we want.

Paula Radcliffe on the treadmill – a great way of exercising indoors.

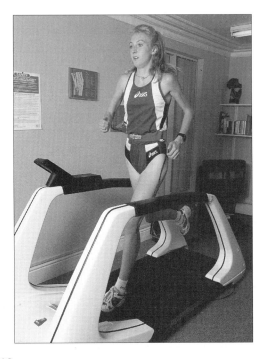

Table 1. Comparison of different sports and their effect on different fitness areas.

Sport	CV	MS	ME	GE	FLEX	DAMAGE
Aerobics	7-9	6	7	6	8	-2
Baseball	3-6	4	5	6	7	-4
Basketball	6-8	7	7	7	7	-4
Bowls	1	3	5	6	6	-1
Cricket	3-6	5	5	7	6	-5
Cycling	7-10	8	9	9	6	-6
Football	6-9	7	7	8	7	-6
Golf	3-4	5	5	6	5	-3
Gymnastics	5-7	8	7	7	10	-4
Hockey	6-8	6	6	7	7	-4
Lacrosse	6-9	6	6	7	7	-3
Rowing	10	8	8	8	5	-2
Running	7-10	5	9	9	5	-2-5
Sailing	2-4	6	7	8	5	-4
Skiing	8-10	7	9	10	6	-4
(downhill)	5-7	6	5	6	7	-7
Squash	6-9	6	6	7	7	-5
Surfing	4-6	7	6	7	7	-3
Swimming	8-10	8	9	8	7	-1
Tennis	5-8	6	6	6	7	-3
Weightlifting	2	10	7	6	7	-3
Yoga	1	5	6	5	10	-1

Notes:

CV = Cardiovascular fitness. The table assumes that all sports are done three or four times a week. If you are only playing once a week, the benefit is only a quarter of that shown. The upper level is an assessment of the effects of playing hard and regularly.

MS = Muscular Strength. This refers to the benefit of doing the sport, rather than training for it.

ME = Muscular Endurance. This refers to the endurance in the muscles used in the sport.

GE = General Endurance or Stamina. This obviously depends on the number of hours of activity per week.

FLEX = Flexibility.

Damage The assessment of the damage factor in a sport depends partly on the frequency of injuries picked up in performing or practising and partly on the risk of accidents associated with the sport. Thus, accidents are quite frequent in skiing and cycling, although the mere performance of the motions rarely leads to injury.

Competition

Why should I compete?

One of the nice things about running is that you are totally in control. You don't need twenty-one other people and a referee. You don't need an opponent. It could be said that nobody needs opponents, that ideally we should all be on the same side. Well, in running you can have it either way. When you run in any kind of race, even if it is only a fun run, you will find that some people are definitely running *against* you, while others are running *with* you. It depends entirely on your attitude to life. Men, in particular, seem to thrive on aggression and competition, while women tend to be more supportive towards one another. The attitude towards competition was best summed up by the late Dr George Sheehan, who wrote some of the wisest and wittiest things about our sport. He said: 'Of course we are not running against each other – we are running against ourselves and we are all witnesses to each other's achievements – but dammit, I just hate to get beaten by another witness in my age group!'

The competitive instinct is a very basic one, and no one reaches a high level in sport without it. My feeling is that it is better to harness it and use it in something healthy, like running, rather than pretend it isn't there. If you are one of those advanced human beings who have grown out of such childish things, then you run to better yourself and you encourage others to do the same.

Joining a group

Whether you are competitive or not, you will get more out of your running if you run with other people. You can share your experiences, encourage one another, get each other out running on days when the weather is bad, and generally provide mutual support for your hopes and ambitions.

It does not have to be anything as formal as a club. We have a staff jogging group at school, called the Kangaroos, because one of the founder members was an Australian, who presented us all with little kangaroo pins. We meet at 7 am on Mondays, Wednesdays and Fridays during term time and run easily for about twenty-five minutes. We don't run fast, we just run along and chat, but we know that there is always someone there to run with, so it gets us out of bed even when it is dark and cold.

The easiest way to start a group is to put up a card on your company's noticeboard or mention it in the firm's news sheet. If you are a housebound parent, new to the neighbourhood, it is more difficult. If you are on your own it might be unwise to advertise the fact. You could get in touch with your nearest leisure centre or community centre and ask if there is a 'Meet and Train' group. If not, you could ask for their help in setting one up. In that way, applications would be filtered through the centre. Once you find a few kindred spirits you can arrange training times to suit you.

Another possible solution, for British women, is to get in touch with the Sister's Network, organized by *Runner's World*. In each area there is a Big Sister who acts as a coordinator for women who want to run on an informal basis. If the group gets bigger, little sisters become big sisters and the number of groups increases. The easiest way, however, is to join a running club.

How to choose a club

You need not feel that you have to be a good runner or a very serious runner to do this. The club is just a group which exists to help the people in it to enjoy the sport as much as possible.

To find where the clubs are based, either go to a running store and ask where the nearest races are, or look in your local paper. You only have to ask a few people at the nearest road race to find out where the clubs are and who to contact – most of them are only too keen to get another member. You don't have to sign up right away – just go along and run with them and if you like the atmosphere you can join.

Do you need a coach?

There is very little skill in running, because it is such a simple and natural activity, so the role of the coach in running is different to that of the coach in ball games. The main roles of a coach of distance runners are:

1. To encourage and support the runner.
2. To advise him on the right training to do.
3. To prevent him from doing too much.
4. To advise him on his racing programme.

The best person to coach you is someone who has a wide experience of the sport; they don't have to be good runners to be good coaches. It is important, though, that you are in touch with them constantly, at least once a week, because the coach has to know the athlete well to know when he should train hard and when he should take it easy. It is important for the runner to keep a training log (see Chapter 2), so that he can tell the coach exactly what is going on.

The great advantage of having a coach is that two minds are far more effective than one when planning a campaign. The coach can give an objective view and the runner learns a lot just by bouncing his ideas off somebody else. When the runner is feeling down the coach must help him up, and when the runner's ambitions are sky-high the coach can help keep his feet on the ground. In the early years, children are often coached by their parents, which works well because the parents know the child better than anyone else does, but

RUNNING IS EASY

In competition, everyone has their own goals. For many, success is completing the course.

there is always the danger of the 'Little League Syndrome' where the parents project their ambitions onto the child and load him up with expectations to an intolerable degree. A better situation is where the club coach controls the overall programme and the parents are asked for support. If they develop a real interest in the sport they can be encouraged to take coaching exams and become involved with the club.

Running-related sports

Apart from road, track, cross-country running and the Marathon, each of which has its own chapter, there are also 'hashing', fell-racing, mountain-running, trail-running, orienteering and the multi-event sports, triathlon, duathlon, tetrathlon and pentathlon.

Fell-racing. This is a specialised form of mountain-running, mostly confined to Scotland and the North of England. It demands particularly strong legs and the kind of nerve more usually associated with cycling than running, but it is still basically a cardiovascular event, demanding a very good oxygen-intake system. The shortest races can be as little as 1000m. In

Cumbria and in Scotland the local grass-track meetings often include a fell race, where the runners take their own route from the track to the top of the fell and back again.

Mountain-running. This term includes fell racing, but also much more. There are all sorts of interesting races in the mountains, particularly in the Alps, the Pyrenees and the Rocky Mountains, which cater for all levels of competition. Some may be over a six or ten-mile distance (10-20km), and some are of marathon duration. At the far end of the scale we have the Swiss Mountain Marathon, which may be 60km or more. Some are just one-off races organized by the local town, but the better-known ones, in Europe, are organized into a race series, the CIME. Many of the runners who emerge from this branch of the sport have the ability to shine on the road or the track. Martin Jones, winner of the World Mountain Cup race, has already represented

England in the Commonwealth Games and Britain in the World Cross-Country Championships. Dave Cannon, a British champion in the mountains, became a successful British international marathon runner. The toughness of this branch of the sport clearly makes it excellent preparation for the more conventional disciplines.

Trail running. This may include mountain running, but is usually a long-distance form of racing, off the road, using forests trails and country paths. In Britain there is the South Downs 80 (miles, not kilometres) which is often run as the World Trail Running Championship, and in the USA there is the Western States Endurance Run, a distance of one hundred miles. These are clearly 'ultra' events, and so are dealt with in Chapter 9, but there are all sorts of un-categorizable races around the world, over all sorts of distances, which do not fall into the more formal structures of track, road and cross-country racing. It is events like these – the Man-versus-Horse race in central Wales, the Mt Kociusko races in Australia, the Up-the-Empire State Building race in New York – which make running so much fun.

Orienteering. This sport evolved in Scandinavia and is still dominated by Scandinavians for whom it is the natural summer alternative to skiing, but it is now genuinely world-wide. It involves running from one control point to another, generally through wooded terrain, navigating with a map and compass. Apart from the fact that it requires above average intelligence, there is little to distinguish the physical demands of orienteering from normal cross-country running. The best cross-country runners do not always make the best orienteers, because the latter need to be particularly self-controlled and clear-headed. Although the average speed of orienteering is lower, it is done over much rougher terrain than cross-country and the events usually last for longer. The best orienteers have to be very good runners, and so their training is on the same lines as that of the cross-country runner, with the additional practice of technical skills.

Orienteering is, above all, great fun. It caters for a very wide range of ability and for older runners it has the advantage that experience and cunning can often prevail against the impetuosity of youth. Each time you find a control the race begins again, so there is always satisfaction to be gained from navigating the next stage. There is often a choice of routes – short and difficult as against long and easy – and whatever your level, there is always the feeling that you could do better next time.

The value of orienteering to runners is considerable and it is very much to be recommended as a form of training, particularly in the build-up period, where general endurance and high-volume cardiovascular training are what you need. The worse your navigation, the more running you do!

Hashing. This is another quirky little corner of the sport where the running is mostly for fun (the other reason is to work up a

Mountain-running – running at its toughest.

duathlon is the most popular, and has championships in its own right, but there are also run-and-swim duathlons and swim-and-bike duathlons.

Triathlon This is by far the most important of the multi-event sports in terms of numbers of athletes and international significance The majority of triathletes centre their training around the Olympic Triathlon distance, which is 1500m swimming, 40km cycling and 10km of running on the road. All three sections are cardiovascular events and put together they demand both general endurance as well as local endurance in different muscles. If you are looking for a sport which requires and develops all-round fitness, you could not do better than triathlon. It has considerable benefits for the 'pure' runner, because the cycling and swimming elements extend his cardiovascular capacity and his leg strength, without putting extra strain on the joints. If the runner is stuck in a rut and feels that he is not improving, I would recommend spending a few months on triathlon training. It will strengthen parts which his running training cannot reach, and he can put in more training per week with less risk of injury. If our 'pure' runner is built exclusively for running, he will probably not be

thirst). The original Hash House Harriers was formed by expatriate Brits in Singapore and Hash clubs flourish all over the world. The idea is to have a sociable run which is followed by a lot of sociable drinking, and the running takes the form of a cross-country run, following a trail laid down by the 'hares', generally marked in sawdust. This is very similar to the paperchases used in Victorian times for cross-country running. It is not done to take the running too seriously, but a lot of fun is had.

Multi-event sports

Biathlon. This term usually refers to the Winter Biathlon, an event in the Winter Olympics which combines cross-country skiing with rifle-shooting. It is mainly an event for the military. The term may sometimes be used as a synonym for Duathlon.

Duathlon. This is a combination of two of the triathlon events. The run-bike-run

Orienteering – the thought sport.

a very successful triathlete because a weak upper body will limit his swimming ability, but he will become a stronger athlete, mentally and physically.

The value of running training for the triathlete is obvious, but the difficult question is what the proportions should be of the different specialities. It makes sense to spend more time on the weakest element, because that will give you the most improvement in your overall time. It also makes sense to have one day a week where you are trying to put all three together,

because you need to simulate competition conditions.

Once you have mastered your cycling skills, more benefit would be gained by concentrating on the other two events for most of the week, but always trying to cover two events per day. Thus one might have two days of hard swim training followed by a run and two days of easy swim training followed by hard running training. The other two days, if one has time, would be swim-cycle and cycle-run, both at well below maximum, and on the seventh day you do all three.

The most effective kind of running training for triathletes would be that recommended for 10km road runners – a combination of interval and repetition running with fast 'aerobic' runs over longer distances.

A typical week's training for Sarah Springman, ten times British triathlon champion, looks like this:

Mon	bike: 24 miles
	swim: 2500m
	bike 12 miles easy
Tue	run: 9 miles steady
	swim: 3500m, inc. 9 x 200 hard
	bike: 22 miles, incl. 4 x 3 miles hard
Wed	bike: 29 miles,
	swim: 2500m
	run: 6 miles, incl. 6 x 700m fast.
Thu	bike: 30 miles, incl. 6 x 1 mile fast
	swim: 3400m, incl. 2200m hard
	interval training
Fri	bike: 18 miles on mountain bike,
	plus 18 miles easy

Multi-terrain running; physically tough, but great fun.

swim: 3000m
run: 4 miles, with bounding and drills.

| Sat | run: 10 miles, incl. 6 mile race |
| Sun | swim: 2500m, incl.10 x 50m, bike 60 miles – fantastic ride! |

Week's total: Swim: 17,500m (6.00 hr)
Bike: 213 miles (12.30 hr)
Run: 29 miles (4 hr)

This was a holiday week, totalling well over twenty hours of training, but such weeks occur frequently in her training diary.

Tetrathlon. This involves horse riding, swimming, pistol shooting and cross-country running. It is really a 'junior' form of Modern Pentathlon and in Britain it is organized mainly by Pony Clubs.

Pentathlon. The original pentathlon was a five-event combination of track and field events. As such it was in the ancient Greek Olympic Games. For many years it was the standard multi-event competition for female athletes in the modern Olympics, until it was superseded by the Heptathlon. The events were 80m hurdles, 200m sprint, High Jump, Long Jump and Shot. This was the event where Mary Peters won her Olympic gold medal in 1972.

Under present-day rules, the Men's Pentathlon consists of 200m, 1500m, Long Jump, Discus and Javelin ,when held outdoors. The Indoor version is 60m hurdles, 1000m, High Jump, Long Jump and Shot Put.

The Women's Pentathlon consists of 100m hurdles, 800m, High Jump, Long Jump and Shot. The indoor version is the same except that the hurdles event is over 60m.

Modern Pentathlon. This is an Olympic event, including horse riding, fencing, pistol shooting, swimming and cross-country running. The running is over a course of 4000m. By its nature, it is an expensive event, unless you happen to be in the Services. It seems likely that it will soon be superseded as an Olympic event by the Triathlon, which has a far more widely-based appeal.

Heptathlon. This consists of seven track and field events. It is now the standard Olympic multi-event competition for female athletes. The events, held over two days are: First day 100m hurdles, High Jump, Shot, 200m. Second day: Long Jump, Javelin, 800m.

Decathlon. This is the standard Olympic multi-event competition for male athletes, the one where Daley Thompson won two Olympic titles. The ten events are: First day: 100m, Long Jump, Shot, High Jump, 400m. Second day: 110m hurdles, Discus, Pole Vault, Javelin, 1500m.

Useful addresses (UK)

Use these to get details of local clubs in the areas which interest you.

British Athletics Federation
225a Bristol Road
Edgbaston
Birmingham B5 7UB
Tel: 0121 440 5000; Fax: 0121 440 0555

Amateur Athletic Association of England
Address as for BAF

Midland Counties AA
3 Duchess Place
Hagley Road
Birmingham B16 8NM
Tel: 0121 452 1500

North of England AA
Suite 106, Emco House
5/7 New York Road
Leeds LS2 7PJ
Tel: 01532 461 835

South of England AA
Suite 36
City of London Fruit Exchange
Brushfield Street
London E1 6EU
Tel: 0171 247 2963

Northern Ireland AAA
House of Sport
Upper Malone Road
Belfast BT9 5LA
Tel: 01232 381 222

Scottish Athletics Federation
Caledonia House
South Gyle
Edinburgh EH12 9DQ
Tel: 0131 317 7322

Athletics Association of Wales
Morfa Stadium
Landore
Swansea
West Glamorgan SA1 7DF
Tel: 01792 456 237

British Orienteering Association
Riversdale
Dale Rd North
Darleydale
Matlock
Derbyshire DE4 2HX
Tel: 01629 734 042

British Olympic Association
1 Wandsworth Plain
London SW18 lET
Tel: 0181 871 2677

British Triathlon Association
PO Box 26
Ashby-de-la-Zouch
Leics LE65 2ZR

Fell Running Association
15 New Park View
Farsley
Leeds LS28 5TZ

Runner's World (for Sisters Network)
7-10 Chandos St
London WlM 0AD
Tel: 0171 291 6000; Fax: 0171 291 6080

Road running

Road running is the heart of the sport. Over ninety per cent of runners consider road running to be their main sport and it is possible to find road races all the year round in almost every country of the world. Because they are not on a track, each one is different and has some feature of interest. There is plenty of room – the field can be as small as half a dozen or as big as fifty thousand. The great advantage of road running is its accessibility, but this can also be a drawback, because the runner may never experience the other branches of the sport until it is too late. I would strongly recommend everyone to try the other disciplines at least once, so that you don't miss out on something for which you have a talent. It is very easy, when you have taken up running, joined your local club and got into the pattern of regular racing, to find that this occupies your time fully. There is nothing wrong with this – it's fun, it is giving you what it should – but don't neglect the other possibilities.

The best thing about running on the roads is that you have a reliable fast surface. It is almost impossible to compare one cross-country time with another, because the weather conditions affect the going underfoot. There might be twenty seconds per kilometre difference between a fast dry course and a really muddy one, but the differences between a good and a bad stretch of road are very slight in terms of running time. Obviously the gradient and the temperature will affect your speed, but once you have got a few regular runs worked out it is easy to see whether you are improving or not just by keeping a record of your times. Similarly, it is easy to find out where you stand, relative to other people, by comparing your times over known distances – five miles, ten kilometres or half-marathon.

Another good thing about running is that, unlike other spheres of life, your efforts are directly rewarded. If you have been following the First Steps Programme, you will be able to see the progress you have made in a short space of time. Look at the Hundred Steps on page 23. What level were you on two years ago? What level are you on now? What level would you like to be on in a year's time?

A very common question is: 'How much do you think I could improve my time for 10 km/marathon?' The answer is that you can only find out by doing it. The improvement you can make depends on how much training you are prepared to do. Everyone has his or her limits, but most of us are a long way from reaching those limits. One thing is certain – you won't reach your limit in your first year of competition. Even the older runner can reckon on three to five years of improvement, as the body gradually changes into a runner's body. Things like the loss of fat, the growth of muscle fibres, an increase in the capillary blood supply or the numbers of enzyme molecules are gradual processes. The body is stressed and then the body responds. Harder training applies more stress and the body responds again. If the stress is too little, no change takes place. If the stress is too much the systems get tired and start to break down.

We may have our limits, but we also have great possibilities of improvement, particularly in the direction of endurance. This is why road running is so enjoyable and so challenging – you can see how your efforts are rewarded, and there are opportunities to run in races of all distances, knowing that there will always be someone of your own age and ability level to run with.

The Club Runner's 10km Programme

Let us assume that you have worked your way up to running regularly on the lines indicated in Chapters 2 and 4 and can run up to 25 miles in a week. You will have probably done one or two fun runs and you want to get fit to run in local races, which will probably be in the 5 miles (8km) to 10km

(6.25 miles) range. The Club Runner's 10km Programme is designed for you. It involves running five times a week, one of which will be with a club group of about your standard and one will be a longer, slower run, probably over the weekend.

The most noticeable difference will be that we are going to introduce the 'quality' sessions outlined in Chapter 4, while maintaining a weekly mileage of about thirty miles a week.

Week 1

Day 1	5 mile run, including 5 x (l min fast, 2 min jog)
Day 2	4 miles steady pace.
Day 3	Club run 6 miles, starting slow, finishing fast.
Day 4	1 mile easy, 3 miles good pace, 1 mile easy.
Day 5	Slow run, 7-8 miles

Week's total: 26 miles approx.

Road racing – Blackheath Harriers lead the way.

Week 2

Day 1	5 miles easy, off road.
Day 2	Warm-up, 6-8 x 45 sec uphill run, cool-down
Day 3	Club run, 6 miles.
Day 4	Warm-up, 2 x 1 mile fast (5 min recovery), cool-down.
Day 5	Slow run, 8 miles.

Week's total: 29 miles approx.

Week 3

Day 1	5 miles, starting slow, finishing fast.
Day 2	1 mile easy, then 8 x 1 min fast, 1 min slow, 1 mile jog.
Day 3	Club run, 6 miles, with a few surges.
Day 4	Warm-up, 1 x 10 min fast, 1 x 5 min fast, 5 min jog.
Day 5	Slow run, off road, 8-10 miles.

Week's total: 28-30 miles approx.

Week 4

Day 1	Warm-up, 4 x 5 min fast, 2 min recovery.
Day 2	5 miles easy, off-road.
Day 3	6 miles club run, with several fast bursts.
Day 4	4-5 miles easy.
Day 5	Race, 5-10 miles – not too serious.

Week's total: 28-33 miles approx

Week 5

Day 1	5-6 miles easy, off-road if possible.
Day 2	Warm-up, 6 x 2 min fast 2 min slow, 6 x 1 min fast 1 min slow, cool-down.
Day 3	Club run, 8 miles good pace.
Day 4	Warm-up, 10 x 45 sec uphill, cool-down.
Day 5	8 miles easy, off-road.

Week's total: 33 miles approx.

Week 6 (Special pre-race week)

Day 1	6 miles fartlek.
Day 2	5 miles easy, off-road.
Day 3	1 mile jog, 10 x 1 min fast, 1 min slow, 2 miles easy.
Day 4	3 mile jog.
Day 5	10km race (with warm-up and cool-down).

Week's total: 29 miles approx.

The Serious Amateurs' 10km Programme

Let us suppose that you have had a couple of seasons of training at about the 'club runner' level. In the first year you improved steadily and in the second year you improved at first, but now the improvement curve has flattened out. You can handle the training alright and you look forward to your races at the weekend, but the times are not getting any faster. If you stay on the same level, your

Liz McColgan, 10,000m champion and New York marathon winner, leading the 1995 Great North Run.

improvement *will* continue, but only very gradually, and once you are past forty the slowing-down caused by age will wipe out the benefits of the continuous training. If you want to improve further, you will have to train harder.

The first step is an increase in volume, without increasing the total amount of hard training. Once you are satisfied that your legs can take the increased mileage, you can put in a higher proportion of hard work. The following programme is based on an average of about 45 miles (75km) a week, so if you are moving up from the Club Runner's Programme you will need

four to six weeks of running 40-45 miles a week before starting on the six-week programme below. While doing this, you should keep in the sessions you were doing before, e.g. 10 x 45 sec uphill and the 4 x 5 min with 2 min recovery.

All interval and repetition sessions, e.g. 15 x 400m, are preceded by 15 min warm-up and followed by 5-15 min cool-down jog.

Week 1

Mon	6 miles steady pace
Tue	15 x 400m (75 sec), 90 sec interval
Wed	5 miles easy, off-road
Thu	6 miles fartlek, on hills
Fri	Rest
Sat	4 x 2000m repetition run, 5 min recovery
Sun	12 miles slow run

Week's total: 45 miles approx.

Week 2

Mon	6 miles, steady pace
Tue	7 miles fartlek
Wed	5 miles easy, off-road
Thu	4 miles brisk pace, with bursts on hills, 1-2 miles easy at end
Fri	Rest or 3 miles jog
Sat	30 min easy, with a few strides
Sun	Race, 5-10 miles

Week's total: 40-45 miles approx.

Week 3

Mon	am 4 miles jog, pm 6 miles steady
Tue	6 x 800m (2 min 30) + 4 x 400m (75 sec), equal time recovery
Wed	5 miles easy
Thu	Hill running, 12 x 45 sec
Fri	Rest or 3 miles jog
Sat	10 min fast, 6 min rest, 5 min fast
Sun	10 miles steady run

Week's total: 45-48 miles approx.

Week 4

Mon	6 miles, start slowly, finish fast
Tue	5 miles easy, off-road
Wed	5 x 1 mile repetition run (4 min rest)
Thu	7 miles slow run
Fri	Rest or 3 miles jog
Sat	5 miles easy fartlek
Sun	Minor race, 3-8 miles

Week's total: 40-45 miles approx.

Week 5

Mon	am 5 miles jog, pm 6-7 miles steady pace
Tue	7-8 miles good pace
Wed	5 miles easy, off-road
Thu	Hill running, 12-14 x 45 sec
Fri	4 miles jog
Sat	20 min hard run, plus warm-up and cool-down
Sun	12-14 miles slowly

Week's total: 50 miles approx.

Week 6 (Pre-race special week)

Mon	7 miles steady, with 8 x 1 min fast, 1 min slow
Tue	6 miles easy, off-road
Wed	10 min fast, 5 min jog, 5 min fast, 3 min jog, 2 min fast
Thu	4 miles jog
Fri	6 miles easy, with strides
Sat	3 miles jog or rest
Sun	10km race

Week's total: 40 miles approx.

Continuation. Once you are racing fit, you can race every week for several weeks, with a single hard session in the middle of the week, or you can race hard every other week, putting in a hard week such as Week 5, followed by an easy pre-race week. This would give a better preparation if you are planning to move up to a half-marathon race.

Elite Runner's 10km Programme

The principles are the same as in the previous programme, but there is an all-round increase in the volume, due partly to training twice a day and partly to increasing the amount of 'quality' running. It is always important to measure this, as well as the total mileage, because it is the quality training which really moves the runner up that extra notch. The advantage of putting in the extra morning runs is that they help the runner to recuperate after the hard sessions, as well as increasing general

It is the 'quality' training that really moves the runner up that extra notch.

endurance. They should not be run hard, but as fast or as slow as you like, just as the body feels. In the second sessions we shall work on a cycle of 'easy-moderate-hard', except when there is a race.

Daily morning run, Monday-Friday, 25-30 min.
Second session as shown below.

Week 1

Mon	5-6 miles easy
Tue	1 mile easy, 4 miles brisk pace, 1 mile jog
Wed	warm-up, 10 x 1 min uphill fast, warm down
Thu	As Monday
Fri	6-7 miles fartlek, bursts of 150-200m
Sat	4 x 2000m on road, 5 min recovery
Sun	10-12 miles easy pace

Week's total: 70miles approx.

Week 2

Mon	5-6 miles easy
Tue	8 miles steady pace, with surges
Wed	Warm-up, 4 x 1 mile, 4 min recovery, warm down
Thu	30 min jog (4 miles approx.)
Fri	5 miles, including 10 x 30 sec fast, 60 sec jog
Sat	Hill training, 6 x 2 min approx.
Sun	12-15 miles easy

Week's total: 70 miles approx.

Week 3

Mon	5-6 miles easy
Tue	6-7 miles steady, with 8 x 150m fast strides
Wed	Interval training, 4 x 400m, 4 x 800m, 4 x 400m, at 5000m pace with 60 sec recovery per 400m, 3 min between sets
Thu	Rest or 30 min jog
Fri	1 mile easy, 4 miles brisk pace, 1 mile jog
Sat	5 x 2000m on road, 4 min recovery
Sun	15 miles steady pace

Week's total: 71-76 miles approx.

Week 4

Mon	5 miles easy
Tue	6 miles fartlek, including 6 x 1 min fast
Wed	6-8 x 1000m fast stride, 2 min recovery
Thu	30 min easy pace
Fri	15 min jog, 8 x 200m fast stride
Sat	30 min jog
Sun	Race, 5-8 miles

Week's total: 56-60 miles approx.

Week 5

Mon	7-8 miles easy pace
Tue	7 miles fartlek
Wed	Hill training, 6 x 2 min approx.
Thu	30 min jog
Fri	2 miles easy, 3 miles good pace, 1 mile jog
Sat	6 x 1200m on grass, 3 min recovery
Sun	15 miles steady pace

Week's total: 70-74 miles approx.

Week 6 (Pre-race week)

Morning runs Mon, Wed and Fri only

Mon	2 miles easy, 3 miles brisk pace, 1 mile easy
Tue	Warm up, 4 x 1200m, race pace (3 min rest)
Wed	7-8 miles steady, with a few surges
Thu	Warm up, 12 x 200m stride (60 sec rest), warm-down
Fri	Morning run only

Sat	20 min run, with strides
Sun	Race

Week's total: 50 miles approx.

Ten miles and Half-marathon

While it is possible to run these distances off a 10km programme, you probably won't reach your ultimate unless you adjust your pace and distance to the longer race. There is no real difference between training for ten miles, which is 16,090 metres, and the half-

The important thing to remember is – enjoy yourself!

marathon, which is 13.1 miles or 21,098 metres. Throughout most of the race you are running at your 'threshold' pace. If you go any faster than this, you start to accumulate lactic acid in your muscles, and you soon feel it. In a half-marathon race, you just have to have the endurance to keep this threshold pace going for twenty kilometres rather than fifteen. In the last kilometre, if you are pushing yourself hard, you will speed up by perhaps ten seconds, but your average speed is going to be much the same. A fast half-marathon course may give you a better ten-mile time than a ten-mile race.

The Beginner's Programme

Beginners should not be running a half-marathon at all. They should run some shorter distances first, so should work their way through the First Steps and the Basic Fitness Programmes in Chapter 2, then try the Club Runner's 10km Programme on p 80. By this time they will have been able to tackle some fun runs and 10km races. Another four weeks on the Club Runner's 10km Programme should provide enough background to try a half-marathon, but they can expect much better results when they have had time to do more training. It is not advisable to move up to the half-marathon distance until they have got used to training at the 40 miles (60km) a week level.

The Club Runner's Programme

This should suit men who are hoping to

run between one hour thirty-something, down to about seventy-eight minutes, for the half-marathon and the equivalent times for women would be between one hour forty and eighty-five minutes. It is based on the assumption that the runner has already been training along the lines of the 10km programme and has therefore got used to running thirty miles (50km) a week.

The six-week programme below should provide enough additional strength to move up to ten miles or half-marathon. If Weeks 3 to 6 are repeated, you should be able to improve still further.

Week 1

Mon	5 miles easy, off-road if possible
Tue	6 miles, fairly fast
Wed	Warm-up, 4 x 3 min fast, with 2 min recoveries
Thu	5 miles easy
Fri	Rest
Sat	1 mile easy, 5 miles fartlek, with bursts on hills
Sun	10 miles steady run

Week's total: 38-40 miles approx.

Week 2

Mon	4-5 miles easy
Tue	6 miles, starting slowly, finishing fast
Wed	Warm up, 3 x 5 min fast, 4 min recoveries
Thu	5 miles easy, with 6 x 100m strides
Fri	Rest or 20 min jog

Sat	Warm up, 1 mile at 10km pace, warm down
Sun	Race over 8-10km, or 8km time trial

Week's total: 32-35 miles approx.

Week 3

Mon	5 miles easy
Tue	Warm up, 16 x 1 min fast, 1 min slow, warm down
Wed	Warm up, 2 x 3000m approx, at 10 mile pace (6 min rest)
Thu	5-6 miles steady pace
Fri	Rest or jog
Sat	Run to hills, 10 x 40 sec uphill fast, jog back
Sun	10 miles steady pace

Week's total: 39-42 miles approx.

Week 4

Mon	5 miles easy, off road
Tue	6 miles steady, with bursts on hills
Wed	Warm up, 3 x 1 mile fast, with 5 min recoveries
Thu	5 miles easy
Fri	Rest or jog
Sat	1-2 miles easy, 4 miles fast, 1-2 miles easy
Sun	10-12 miles slow run or minor race

Week's total: 40-43 miles approx.

Week 5

Mon	5 miles steady, with a few strides
Tue	2 x 3000m approx, timed, as Week 3
Wed	6 miles steady
Thu	Run to hill, 12 hill climbs as Week 3, jog back
Fri	Rest or 20 min jog
Sat	6 miles including 10 x 1 min fast, 1 min slow, 10 x 30 sec fast, 30 sec slow
Sun	8 miles steady, with a few surges

Week's total: 37-40 miles approx.

Week 6

Mon	5 miles easy, off road
Tue	6-7 miles at a comfortable pace, plus 6 x 100m strides
Wed	Warm-up, 2 miles at race pace, 2 miles jog
Thu	5 miles easy, with 8 x 30 sec fast, 60 sec jog
Fri	Rest
Sat	3 miles jog, in racing kit
Sun	Race day

Week's total: Doesn't matter.

The Serious Amateur's Programme

This is designed for those aiming at times below 78 min (men) or 85 min (women) for a half-marathon. It is still based on training once a day. The mileage goes up to 50 a week (80km), and as well as the repetitions and intervals, there is more emphasis on fast continuous running. I am assuming that those following the schedule have already gone through the corresponding 10km programme given above. The speed

Follow the schedule and you should find that your times improve dramatically.

of your best training should be around 5km pace for the short runs (up to 800m), at 10km pace for the runs over 1000 to 2000m and at ten mile pace for the longer repetitions and fast tempo runs, because that corresponds to your 'threshold pace'.

Week 1

Mon	6 miles easy, off road if possible
Tue	6-7miles fartlek, with bursts up the hills
Wed	6 miles easy
Thu	6-7 miles, including 10 x 1 min fast, 1 min slow and 6 x 30 sec fast, 30

sec slow

Fri	Rest or 3 mile jog
Sat	1 mile easy, 6 miles fast, 1 mile easy
Sun	10-12 miles easy run

Week's total: 42-49 miles approx

Week 2

Mon	6 miles easy
Tue	6-7 miles, incl. 6 x 2 min fast, 2 min slow
Wed	6 miles, starting easy, finishing fast
Thu	Interval training, 12 x 400m fast, 90 sec recovery, or 16 x 1 min fast, 1 min slow
Fri	3 miles jog
Sat	Warm up, 4-5 miles fast timed run, warm down
Sun	10 miles steady run

Week's total: 45 miles approx

Week 3

Mon	6 miles easy, off road
Tue	3 x 2 miles, with 5 min recovery jog
Wed	6 miles easy
Thu	8 miles fartlek on grass, with lots of 30 sec bursts
Fri	3 miles jog
Sat	5 miles (easy pace if racing)
Sun	13 miles steady, or warm-up plus race, 8-10km

Week's total: 45-49 miles approx

Week 4

Mon	6 miles easy

Tue	7-8 miles hilly fartlek, with bursts up the hills
Wed	6 miles steady pace
Thu	6 x 1 mile (or 6 x 5 min), with 4 min recoveries
Fri	3 miles jog
Sat	5-6 miles on grass, with strides
Sun	15 miles slow run

Week's total: 50-53 miles approx

Week 5

Mon	5 miles easy, off road
Tue	3 x 2 miles, as Week 3, but faster
Wed	5 miles easy
Thu	Warm up, then 2 sets of 8 x 200m on grass, short recovery
Fri	3 miles jog
Sat	Warm-up, then 4-5 miles timed run, as Week 2
Sun	12-14 miles easy pace

Week's total: 46-48 miles approx

Week 6

Mon	5 miles easy, off road
Tue	6-8 miles easy
Wed	Warm up, 2 x 1 mile at race pace, warm down
Thu	Warm up, 10 x 200m fast on grass, 60 sec recovery
Fri	Rest or jog
Sat	Jog 3 miles, in racing kit
Sun	Race day

Week's total: Doesn't matter.

The International Programme

This is designed for those aiming to run 65 minutes or faster (men) and 71 minutes or faster (women). The runners will already have been training at a high level and racing over 10km in road and cross-country races, but there is an extra dimension of stamina required here. There are runners for whom the 20 km/half-marathon distance is ideal. They are not quite fast enough to win big races over 10km and they lack the special mental and physical qualities of a marathon runner.

Fortunately, there are now enough races in the 15-25km distance to give them a chance to shine; these include such big 'halves' as the Milan Stramilano, the Great North Run and the Tokyo, Gothenburg and Lisbon races. There is now an annual World (Half-Marathon) Championships, for individuals and teams, which gives the ambitious road racer something to aim for.

It is for people such as this that this schedule is devised. It differs from the marathon schedule only in not including long runs of more than 30km (19 miles). The top class marathon runner needs as much fast running as the half-marathon man or woman, but he also needs a bigger endurance base. The half-marathon runner is training for an event which lasts for just over an hour, so although he may be training for two hours a day quite often, the crucial sessions are those where he is making a hard effort for 40-60 minutes.

Daily run of 4-5 miles unless specifically omitted.

Second session as shown. (NB For women, where speeds are shown, e.g. 6 min/mile, the women's target speed will be approximately ten per cent slower, i.e. 6.6 min or 6 min 36 sec.)

Week 1

Mon	7-8 miles steady (6 min/mile, 3.45/km)
Tue	10 miles run, incl 6 x 5 min fast, 3 min jog
Wed	6 miles easy
Thu	10 x 1000m in 2.55, 2 min recovery
Fri	Morning run only
Sat	10 miles cross-country, good 'aerobic' pace (sub-6 min/mile)
Sun	18 miles at comfortable pace. No early morning run

Week's total: 85-90 miles approx

Week 2

Mon	7-8 miles fartlek
Tue	2 x (10 x 400m) on track, 65-67 sec, 30 sec recovery, plus 3 min jog between sets
Wed	5 miles easy, off road
Thu	3 x 2 miles on road (or 3 x 10 min), 5 min rests
Fri	Morning run only
Sat	10 miles easy fartlek
Sun	Minor road race (10km) plus 4 x 1 mile at same tempo, 3 min rests. No morning run

Week's total: 80 miles approx.

Week 3

Mon	10 miles, easy pace
Tue	8 x 1200m at 10km pace, 2-3 min recovery
Wed	6 miles, easy on grass
Thu	Hill running, incl 6 x 3 min uphill, hard.
Fri	Morning run only
Sat	2 x 5km 'tempo' run, at 3.00/km
Sun	18-20 miles at comfortable pace. No second run.

Week's total: 86-90 miles approx

Week 4

Mon	7-8 miles easy fartlek
Tue	6 x (800m + 400m) at 65-66 sec, 60 sec recovery between the 800m and 400m, 200m jog in 90 sec after the 400.
Wed	6 miles steady run
Thu	2 x (8 x 200m) on grass, untimed
Fri	5 miles easy
Sat	Morning run only
Sun	Race, 10km or 10 miles. No early run

Week's total: 70-75 miles approx

Week 5

Mon	8 miles steady
Tue	5 miles fartlek
Wed	2 x (10 x 400m), as Week 2. No early run
Thu	5 miles easy on grass
Fri	Morning run only
Sat	2 x 8km tempo run, at 3.00/km, 10 min rest.
Sun	14-15 miles steady pace (6 min/mile). No early run

Week's total: 75 miles approx.

Week 6 (Pre-race – early morning runs Mon and Wed only)

Mon	6 miles easy fartlek
Tue	Long warm-up, 2 x 1 mile at race pace, in racing shoes
Wed	5 miles easy
Thu	Warm-up, 8 x 200m stride, 60 sec recovery
Fri	3 miles jog
Sat	3 miles jog, in racing kit
Sun	Race day

Week's total: Doesn't matter.

Chapter 8

The marathon

If you stand outside the Olympic museum in Lausanne looking towards the lake, the view is very attractive – children playing on the grass, the trees beside the lake, the boats on the water. Then you lift your eyes above the trees and the boats and there, thousands of feet above the lake and framed against a sky of the palest blue, is the immense mountain wall of the Matterhorn, its peaks dusted with snow. That is how the marathon seems to the ordinary runner – a hard, high and lonely place, the ultimate challenge. You feel that those who have met that challenge, like those who have climbed the highest mountains, will never be quite the same again – and you may be right.

Physiologically, running a marathon is just outside the grasp of the ordinary man or woman. I'm not talking about just getting round in five or six hours – though that in itself is something to achieve – but actually running it to the best of your ability. The magic figure of three hours is something achieved by less than ten per cent of the men running in the London Marathon. This is a performance which represents a peak of achievement for the 'club' level runner, and the female equivalent time would be around 3 hours and twenty minutes.

However, just as climbing the Matterhorn, once a pinnacle of achievement, is now a routine climb, so running a marathon is achievable, even if it not easy.

At least there is a well-marked route and there are guidebooks – this is one of them. So, to pursue the climbing analogy, I want you to fix your eyes on the summit and ignore the bodies of those who have dropped out along the way. If you want to run a marathon, the first thing you need is commitment and the second is common-sense, to prevent yourself from going to far too soon.

The reason that this distance, 42,195 metres or 26 miles 385 yards, presents such a problem is that we only have enough readily available energy stores to run fifteen to twenty miles, even if we are fit enough to take the muscular fatigue. When we run, say, a ten-mile race, we are mainly using up the glycogen which is stored in our muscles and our liver. This is broken down into glucose, the preferred fuel for muscle fibres. Once this supply of glucose runs low, the body has to switch over to using more and more fat, of which even the skinniest of us have ample reserves. If we continue to push ourselves hard when the glucose is already low, we start to get dizzy spells and even hallucinations, because the brain cells, which rely totally on glucose, are being deprived of their usual food. The feeling of weakness and the collapse which often follows is known to runners as 'hitting the wall'.

I have experienced it myself, once. It is not pleasant. All you can do is drop to a shuffle and run at about two-thirds of your normal speed. You can keep going alright on fat, but you have to go much more slowly, because the fat molecules need more oxygen to break them down.

All this can be avoided simply by running more slowly from the start. When you run really fast, i.e. at your 10km racing speed, you are burning 100% glucose, but when you are jogging your muscles are burning up a proportion of fat, and so your glycogen supply lasts longer. There are ways in which you can make yourself a more efficient runner by training, and there are ways in which you can increase the amount of glucose available to you in the race.

The human body is tremendously adaptable, as long as you give it time. When I ran from Los Angeles to New York, I was running the marathon distance every morning, in about three-and-a-half hours, and after a couple of hours rest I was doing another twenty-odd miles in the afternoon. It is just a matter of getting used to it.

Training for the marathon

In the schedules below you should find a programme to suit your ability, but everyone has to make up his own schedule and his own target, because everyone is different. Following the sub-three-hour schedule will only make you run a sub-three-hour marathon if you have the ability to do it. The schedules are arranged in order of increasing effort, so it would be a good idea in your first year to select one of the less strenuous programmes and see what you can do on that. If you have the enthusiasm to do another one, then you can re-assess yourself and perhaps set your standards a little higher next time.

Assessing yourself

Be honest. Do you just want to get round, however slow the speed? If that is the case, and you can only afford a little time during the week, follow my minimal schedule. If you feel that you are prepared to put more into it, you have to assess what you are capable of and how much time you are prepared to spend on training.

Running ability depends partly on training and partly on inherited features. The power-to-weight ratio is very important. If you

A marathon start. Avoid falling over and settle into your race pace as soon as possible.

weigh two hundred pounds you will never be a top class marathon runner, because larger bodies generate more heat and there is not enough surface area to dissipate the heat. Moreover, the heavier you are, the greater the impact forces on the knees and ankles and the greater the danger of injury. Such features as your muscle type – the proportion of slow-twitch and fast-twitch fibres – your heart-lung capacity and even the amount of fat in your body are dictated largely by genetic features. Training can modify them but it cannot alter them very much.

Most people will have some idea about how good they are at running, but that idea may have been laid down right back in the early teens, since when many changes have occurred. The only way you will find out is by getting into running and getting yourself fit to race. From the speed that you can run over ten kilometres we can get a good idea of your marathon potential. Your best running speed for a marathon is going to be about twenty per cent slower than your flat-out mile speed, or about ten per cent slower than your speed for ten kilometres or six miles.

If you take 40 minutes to run 10km, that is 4 min per kilometre. Ten per cent slower than that is 4.4 min per kilometre, or 185 minutes for the marathon distance – three hours five.

If you take 40 minutes to run 6 miles, that is 6.66 min per mile, and ten percent onto that is 7.33 min per mile (7 min 20 sec), which gives us 192 minutes for the marathon – three hours 12 minutes. All

this assumes that you will have done the stamina training, so that your muscles will stand up to running on the road for that distance. Table 2 gives an estimate of how your times for the 10 kilometres and half-marathon will equate to a full marathon.

Table 2. Hour times for 10km and half-marathon equate to a full marathon

10km time	Half-marathon time	Marathon time
30.00	65.00	2h 19.15
32.00	69.10	2h 28.30
35.00	75.30	2h 42.00
37.30	82.00	2h 55.00
40.00	90.00	3h 05.00
44.00	99.00	3h 31.00
48.00	108.00	3h 50.00
50.00	112.30	4h 01.00
55.00	124.00	4h 26.00

Laying the foundations

Having fixed a goal, you need to decide how many hours a week or miles a week you are prepared to put in and you can see on the schedules below how much training is needed. If you are prepared to put in fifty miles a week, which is about eight or nine hours of running, then you should think of working your way gradually up to that mileage, without worrying about the speed. Give yourself at least one easy week out of every four, so that your body has time to adjust to the extra load. Since the schedules run for sixteen weeks,

Elite Women's Start, London Marathon. Some of these runners are showing too much tension.

involved in other sports, may not find this necessary. It should give you the fitness to get around in under five hours, even allowing for a bit of walking.

Since we are not worried about the speed, there will be very little fast running in this schedule. We should concentrate on building up your endurance without getting injured, and if at the same time we can cut down your body weight a little you will find running much easier. You can follow this one even if you have not been through the First Steps Programme, but I would advise you to do the stretching exercises regularly (see Appendix A).

you could build up to running the marathon in less than six months, assuming that you are already fairly fit and running regularly.

The 'Get-you-round' schedule

This is just what it says. The person following it has not got the time or the inclination to do the full training schedule, but wants to prove something by covering the marathon distance. Even with this programme, he will make a big improvement in fitness and probably lose some weight. The biggest danger is that, lacking a running background, his musculo-skeletal system – particularly the knees and ankles – may not be strong enough to take the longer runs. A month of regular walking, with a couple of miles every day and walks of one to two hours each weekend, will help in this respect, but those who are young and strong and who are already

Week 1

Day 1.	20 min jogging each day. You are allowed to stop and walk, but the walking time does not count.
Day 2.	
Day 3.	
Day 4.	One hour of jogging and walking, no pressure

Week 2

Day 1.	
Day 2.	20-25 min jogging on each day
Day 3.	
Day 4.	80-90 min of jogging and walking

Week 3

Day 1.	
Day 2.	20-25 min jogging daily
Day 3.	
Day 4.	90 min jogging and walking

Week 4

Day 1.	20 min jogging
Day 2.	25 min jogging
Day 3.	15 min continuous run
Day 4.	One hour of training, trying to run for 10 min, walk for 5 min, run for 10 min and so on

Week 5

Day 1.	20 min run
Day 2.	20-25 min jog, with several faster bursts
Day 3.	Timed run over 2 miles approx.
Day 4.	10km road race, or 90 min walk-jog

Week 6

Day 1.	25-30 min run
Day 2.	Warm up, then 8 x 30 sec uphill fast
Day 3.	25-30 min steady
Day 4.	One hour of mostly jogging

Week 7

Day 1	30 min run
Day 2.	30 min run, including 6 x 1 min fast, 2 min jog
Day 3.	25 min brisk run
Day 4.	30 min steady run
Day 5.	8 miles run, walking when you have to

Week 8

Day 1.	30 min run
Day 2.	30 min run, including bursts of 30 sec and 60 sec, interspersed with jogging
Day 3.	25 min brisk run, including one timed mile
Day 4.	Half-marathon race or 2 hours jogging-walking

Week 9

Day 1.	30 min steady run
Day 2.	Warm-up, 2 x 1 mile, timed, with a 5 min rest
Day 3.	30 min steady
Day 4.	30 min steady, working harder up the hills
Day 5.	8 miles, as Week 7, but faster

Week 10

Day 1.	25-30 min easy
Day 2.	Timed run over 3 miles approx.
Day 3.	25-30 min easy
Day 4.	25-30 min, with several 30-sec bursts
Day 5.	10 mile run – take it slowly

Week 11

Day 1.	25-30 min easy, off road if possible
Day 2.	Warm up, 3 x 1 mile, timed
Day 3.	25-30 min easy
Day 4.	20-25 min brisk run
Day 5.	Ten-mile race or 1 hr 45 min slow run

Week 12

Day 1.	25-30 min easy
Day 2.	3 mile timed run
Day 3.	20 min steady
Day 4.	25-30 min, or rest if racing
Day 5.	Half-marathon race or two-hour run with friends

Week 13

Day 1.	20 min easy run
Day 2.	3 x 1 mile, timed, as Week 11
Day 3.	20 min easy run
Day 4.	35 min run at marathon pace
Day 5.	16-18 mile endurance run. Go easily, walk 5 min in each hour

Week 14

Day 1.	20 min easy
Day 2.	Timed 3 mile run, as Week 12
Day 3.	40 min run at marathon pace
Day 4.	20 min easy
Day 5.	10 mile run or race 6-10 miles

Week 15

Day 1.	20 min easy run
Day 2.	35 min at marathon pace
Day 3.	2 x 1 mile, timed
Day 4.	20 min easy
Day 5.	50 min at marathon pace. Practice your pre-race preparation

Week 16

Mon	20 min easy
Tue	Warm up, l mile at marathon pace, in racing kit.
Wed	20 min easy, with a few strides
Thu/Fri	Rest
Sat	20 min easy, in racing kit
Sunday	The Race

The Serious Amateur Programme

This is for the person who already has a few years of running background. He or she may not expect ever to reach national class, but all the same would like to run a 'decent' marathon, somewhere in the three to three-and-a-half hour range, while coping with the demands of normal life. For most of us this means running over forty miles a week but not more than sixty. It can be done, thousands do it every year in the big city marathons, but it is not easy. The big problem is really mental – how to keep up the training week after week, particularly the longer runs. This is where you need support – friends to run with you, or someone to come out on a bike – and you should always try to arrange this well in advance.

Chapter
8

Week 1

Mon	5 miles easy
Tue	6 miles. Start slowly, finish faster
Wed	Jog 1 mile, then run 10 x (1 min fast, 2 min slow)
Thu	6 miles easy
Fri	Rest
Sat	5-7 miles steady, off road
Sun	8 miles steady

Total: 37-39 miles

Week 2

Mon	5 miles easy
Tue	1 mile easy, 3 miles faster, 1 mile easy
Wed	6 miles steady
Thu	1 mile warm-up, then 4 x 3 min fast, 2 min slow
Fri	Rest
Sat	6 miles easy
Sun	10 miles slow

Total: 38 miles

Week 3

Mon	5 miles easy
Tue	6 miles steady, with a few faster strides
Wed	Run to hills, then 8 x 40 sec uphill fast, jog back
Thu	5 miles easy
Fri	Rest
Sat	6-8 miles, grass or cross-country
Sun	12 miles easy

Total: 40-42 miles

Week 4

Mon	5 miles steady
Tue	Warm up, then 3 x 1000m, with 3 min recovery. Warm down
Wed	5 miles easy
Thu	Run to hill, 9 x 40 sec uphill fast, jog back
Fri	Rest
Sat	Warm up, 3 miles brisk, warm down
Sun	10 miles, as Week 2, but more strongly

Total: 37 miles

Week 5

Mon	5 miles easy
Tue	6 miles, starting slowly, then putting in 200m bursts, with about 400m recovery jog after each
Wed	Warm up, 3 x 1 mile, timed at about half-marathon pace
Thu	6 miles, starting slowly, finishing faster
Fri	Rest or 3 mile jog
Sat	30 min easy
Sun	Half-marathon race or 15 miles steady

Total: 42-45 miles

Week 6

Mon	5 miles easy, off road
Tue	6 miles, starting slowly, finishing faster
Wed	Hill session, as Week 4, but do one more

Thu	7 miles steady, with some fast strides at the end
Fri	3 miles jogging
Sat	5 miles fartlek, with some fast 200m bursts
Sun	13 miles, easy pace

Total: 45 miles

Week 7

Mon	5 miles easy
Tue	3 x 10 min, at half-marathon pace, with 4 min rests
Wed	4 miles easy
Thu	6 miles steady, with a few surges
Fri	Rest
Sat	Warm up, 3 miles brisk pace, warm down
Sun	18 miles, long slow run. Practice taking drinks

Total: 45 miles

Week 8

Mon	4 miles easy, off road
Tue	5 miles easy
Wed	Warm up, 4 x 1 mile, timed
Thu	6 miles steady
Fri	Rest or 3 miles easy
Sat	5 miles steady, with a few fast strides
Sun	Half-marathon race, or 15 miles steady

Total: 42-45 miles

Week 9

Mon	5 miles easy, off road
Tue	6 miles, putting in bursts if you feel good
Wed	Run to hills, then 10 x 40 sec fast uphill, jog back
Thu	6 miles, starting slowly.
Fri	Rest
Sat	Warm up, 4 miles brisk pace, warm down
Sun	16-17 miles endurance run – take it steady

Total: 45 miles

Week 10

Mon	5 miles easy, off road
Tue	5 miles easy, with some fast strides
Wed	8 miles steady, mostly at marathon pace
Thu	6 miles fartlek, putting in 30 sec bursts with 60 sec recovery after each
Fri	Rest or 3 mile jog
Sat	6 miles steady, including 3 miles fast if not racing
Sun	11-13 miles steady or race 10-13 miles

Total: 44-46 miles

Week 11

Mon	5 miles easy
Tue	Warm up, then 10 x 400m fast, 2 min recovery, or 12 x 1 min fast, 2 min slow, warm down
Wed	8 miles at marathon pace
Thu	6 miles, starting slowly, finishing faster

Fri	Rest
Sat	5 miles easy, with a few strides
Sun	18 miles endurance run, as Week 7 but a bit faster

Total: 48 miles

Week 12

Mon	5 miles easy, off road
Tue	5 miles easy
Wed	Warm up, 4 x 1 mile timed, as Week 8, but faster.
Thu	6 miles steady
Fri	Rest
Sat	4 miles jogging, with easy strides
Sun	Half-marathon race

Total: 44 miles

Week 13

Mon	5 miles easy, off road
Tue	6 miles steady
Wed	6 miles fartlek, as Week 10
Thu	8 miles, including 2 x 3 miles at marathon pace
Fri	3 miles jogging and striding
Sat	Rest
Sun	18-20 miles endurance run

Total: 48 miles

Week 14

Mon	4 mile jog, off road
Tue	8 miles steady
Wed	Warm up, 6 x 800m fast (2 min rests) or 6 x 3 min fast

Thu	6 miles easy
Fri	Rest
Sat	7 miles, incl. 5 miles, timed, at marathon pace
Sun	10-12 miles, with 6 miles fast, or race 10km

Total: 45 miles

Week 15

Mon	5 miles easy, off road
Tue	6 miles steady
Wed	Warm up, 10 x 400m fast, with 90 sec recoveries
Thu	5 miles easy
Fri	Rest
Sat	Warm up, 3 miles at marathon pace
Sun	10 miles steady. Practice your pre-race preparation.

Total: 39 miles

Week 16

Mon	4 miles easy, off road
Tue	Warm up, 2 x 1 mile, timed, at race pace, warm down
Wed	4 miles easy, with a few strides
Thu	3 miles easy, in marathon kit
Fri	Rest
Sat	20 min easy, in marathon kit
Sun	The Race

Total: Forget it!

London Marathon mass start. If you are back in the field, ignore your time for the first mile, but try to settle into your pace after that.

National Level Programme

This programme is designed for the good club runner who has decided to have a serious go at the marathon. The mileage is not particularly high until the runs through the weekend start getting really long, but there is plenty of quality. I believe that a marathon runner should train like a 10km runner, but with added endurance. Unlike the 'international' schedule which follows, I am assuming that the runner has a full-time job. My feeling is that this level of training will take the talented male runner below 2 hr 30 in the first year and below 2 hr 20 in the following year; the equivalent figures for women would be 2.45 and 2.35.

If your goals are not as high as this, say in the 2.45 to 3.00 range (men) or 3.00 to 3.18 (women), I suggest that you follow a slightly scaled down version of this programme. Cutting out the morning runs on Mondays and Wednesdays would reduce your mileage by 8-10 miles a week, while retaining all the quality work.

Week 1

Mon	am 4 miles easy, pm 5 miles steady
Tue	4 x 1 miles at 10km pace, 3 min recovery
Wed	am 4 miles easy, pm 6 miles steady
Thu	2 x (8x 200m) fast stride, 40 sec between strides, 3 min between sets
Fri	5 miles easy
Sat	5-6 miles brisk pace
Sun	13-15 miles easy pace

Week's total: 55-57 miles

Week 2

Mon, Wed, Fri mornings – 4 miles easy

Mon	5 miles steady
Tue	Run to hill, 12 x 40 sec fast uphill, jog down recovery
Wed	6 miles steady
Thu	Interval training, track or grass. 6 x 800m (2 min recovery plus 6 x 400m (1 min recovery) at 5km speed

Fri	Morning run only
Sat	6 miles easy
Sun	Warm-up, 10km race, long cool-down

Week's total: 55 miles

Week 3

Mon, Wed, Fri, 5 miles in morning or at lunchtime

Mon	6 miles starting slowly, finishing quickly
Tue	Repetition session, 1 x 2 miles, 4 x 1 mile (as for Week 1)
Wed	6 miles steady
Thu	7-8 miles fartlek
Fri	Morning run only
Sat	3 miles easy
Sun	16-18 miles, easy pace

Week's total: 62-64 miles

Week 4

Mon, Wed, Fri, 5 miles as Week 3

Mon	5 miles easy, with 6 x 150m fast stride at end
Tue	8 x 1000m (track or grass), 2 min recoveries
Wed	6 miles steady
Thu	14 x 40 sec hill run, as Week 2
Fri	Morning run only
Sat	4 miles easy
Sun	Half-marathon race

Week's total: 62-64 miles

Week 5

Mon, Wed, Fri, 5 miles morning run, easy pace

Mon	6 miles, starting slowly, finishing faster, plus 6 x 150m strides
Tue	7-8 miles fartlek
Wed	Repetition runs, 3 x 2 miles (5-6 min rest)
Thu	6 miles steady, plus 8 x 100m strides
Fri	Morning run only
Sat	3-5 miles jog
Sun	18-20 miles easy run

Week's total: 66-68 miles

Week 6

Mon, Wed, Fri – 5 miles morning run, easy pace

Mon	6 miles, starting slowly, with 8 x 150m strides at end
Tue	Interval training, 2 x (10 x 400m) at 5km pace, 60 sec between runs, 3 min between sets.
Wed	4 miles steady
Thu	Long hills, 6 x 2 min uphill, jog down recovery
Fri	Morning run only
Sat	4-5 miles easy, plus strides
Sun	Race or time trial over 10-13 miles

Week's total: 62-64 miles

Week 7

Three morning runs totalling 15 miles

Mon	6 miles steady
Tue	Repetition runs, 1 x 2 miles, 4 x 1 mile, as for Week 3
Wed	6 miles easy, off road
Thu	8-9 miles at threshold pace
Fri	4 miles easy
Sat	5 miles easy, plus strides, 8 x 100m
Sun	22-24m long slow run. Take drinks en route

Week's total: 77-79 miles

Week 8

Three morning runs totalling 15 miles

Mon	4 miles easy, off road
Tue	6 miles steady
Wed	Interval training, track or grass. 10 x 800m at 10km pace with 90 sec recovery
Thu	6 miles steady, plus 6 x 100m strides
Fri	4 miles easy
Sat	5 miles easy, with 1 mile at race pace, for practice
Sun	Half-marathon race, long warm-up and cool-down

Week's total: 65 miles

Week 9

Three morning runs, totalling 15 miles

Mon	6 miles slow, off road

Tue	Repetition runs, 4 x 1 mile (3 min rest)
Wed	6 miles easy, off road
Thu	8 miles fartlek, with several good bursts
Fri	3 miles jog
Sat	Rest
Sun	27-29 miles, slowly, taking drinks

Week's total: 75 miles

Week 10

Three morning runs, totalling 15 miles

Mon	5 miles easy, off road
Tue	6 miles, starting slowly
Wed	8 miles good pace, with surges if you feel good
Thu	8 miles run with 10-12 x 90 sec fast, 90 sec slow
Fri	4 miles jog
Sat	6 miles fartlek, easy if racing
Sun	10km minor race, or 12 miles run at around marathon pace

Week's total: 64 miles

Week 11

Three morning runs totalling 15 miles

Mon	8 miles brisk run, threshold pace
Tue	6 miles easy fartlek
Wed	Long hills session, 7-8 x 2 min uphill, as for Week 6
Thu	6-8 miles, starting slowly, finishing strongly
Fri	4 miles jog

Sat	Rest
Sun	22-24 miles endurance run, just below marathon pace

Week's total: 75 miles

Week 12

Three morning runs, totalling 15 miles

Mon	5 miles jog, off road
Tue	6 miles steady
Wed	Interval training, 2 x (8-10 x 400m) at 5km pace, as for Week 6
Thu	5 miles easy
Fri	Rest
Sat	4 miles jogging and striding
Sun	Half-marathon run at marathon pace, or race

Week's total: 60 miles

Week 13

Three morning runs, totalling 15M

Mon	5 miles easy, off road
Tue	6 miles easy fartlek
Wed	3 miles marathon pace, 1 mile jog, 3 miles at 10 sec/mile faster
Thu	7 miles steady, plus 8 x 150m strides
Fri	4 miles jog
Sat	Rest
Sun	22-24 miles endurance run as Week 11, different course

Week's total: 70 miles

Week 14

Three morning runs totalling 15 miles

Mon	5 miles easy, off road
Tue	6-7 miles, starting slow, finishing strongly
Wed	8 x 1000m (2 min rest)
Thu	8 miles, mostly at marathon pace
Fri	Rest or 30 min easy
Sat	4 miles jogging, plus 6 x 100m strides
Sun	Race, 6-10 miles

Week's total: 62-65 miles

Week 15

Morning runs on Mon and Wed only

Mon	6 miles easy, off road
Tue	6 miles fartlek, with 8 x 1 min fast, 2 min slow
Wed	1 mile easy, 4-5 miles brisk pace, 1 mile jog
Thu	6 mile easy
Fri	Rest
Sat	Marathon warm-up, 10km at marathon pace, cool-down
Sun	10-12 miles, slow and easy

Week's total: 55 miles

Week 16

Mon	am 3 miles easy, pm 5 miles easy, plus strides
Tue	Warm up, 1 mile at race pace, cool down

Wed	am 3 miles jog, pm 30 min easy, plus strides
Thu	3 miles easy, in racing kit
Fri	Rest
Sat	30 min jog, in racing kit, with easy strides.
Sun	The Race day

Week's total: Forget it!

The International Programme

If you are prepared to do everything you can to reach the highest level, this is your schedule. The distances covered go up to 120 miles (190km) a week, which is not unusual amongst the best marathon men. Some men and even some women get up to 150 miles (240km) at the biggest weeks, but to maintain this for long is dangerous, I believe. The principle – training like a 10,000m runner with added endurance – still holds, but the extra distances make for a better aerobic base as well as increasing the powers of endurance.

It is hard to tell directly what changes are going on inside the athlete's body during the training processes. The successful marathon runner needs to have a large carbohydrate store but he also needs to be efficient at converting fat. The thing to bear in mind is that training is very specific. If you want to be able to run a marathon in 2 hours and 8 minutes or less, you have got to get used to running 5 kilometres in fifteen minutes.

At this level, you are planning for a particular athlete to run in a particular race, so you start by drawing up a general plan, working backwards from the race day, inserting the major races, the time to be spent at altitude and the travelling required. If one is planning a 12-week specific preparation – bearing in mind that the athlete will already be very fit – one has to include at least six long runs; these, along with the other fixed points, form a framework into which the other necessary ingredients must be fitted. The framework will look like this:

Manuela Machado (Portugal), European and World marathon champion.

Weeks to go	Event	Remarks
12	Long run	
11	Race	
10	Long run	
9	Race	Travel to altitude camp
8	Long run	At altitude
7	Long run	At altitude
6	Long run	At altitude
5	Long run	Return from altitude
4	Race	
3	Long run	
2	Race/Trial	Start tapering
1		Tapering, diet control, travel to venue
0	Race Day	

Sun	am Long run, 21 miles in 2 hr, pm swim
Mon	am 5 miles easy, swim, pm 6 miles easy, plus strides
Tue	am 10 miles good pace, pm 6 miles steady
Wed	am 10 x 3 min uphill, pm 6 miles easy, swim
Thu	am 6 miles easy, pm 6 miles steady, plus exercises
Fri	am 8 miles fartlek, pm 7 miles steady
Sat	am 2 x (10 x 400m) on track, pm 6 miles easy
Sun	Single run, 15-16 miles, plus swimming
Mon	am 6 miles steady, pm 6 miles with surges
Tue	am brisk 'aerobic' 10 miles, pm 6 miles steady, swim
Wed	am 10 x 1000m off road, pm 6 miles steady
Thu	am 4 miles easy, swim, pm 5 miles easy, swim
Fri	am 8 miles, including 16 fast hill climbs, pm 6 miles
Sat	am 5 miles easy, pm 5 miles with strides
Sun	am Long run, 24 miles, pm swim

Each race will require a couple of easy days beforehand and each long run will require an easy day after it.

The next thing is to put down the ingredients to be put into each phase of the training. Some coaches will prefer to start with a lot of endurance work and then proceed to faster and shorter training. I prefer to concentrate on high-quality training sessions in the first six weeks, using road races for their combination of hard workout and gaining tactical experience. Even a 12-week training period should not proceed without a break, so I schedule an easy week, which will precede either a race or the beginning of the altitude period. A two-week cycle of training in this phase will look like this:

Total for 2 weeks: 205 miles

After adjustment to altitude, which will only take five days for an experienced distance runner, we switch to more

106

marathon-related training, but still use the occasional track session as a check on fitness. The training in a typical week would look like this:

Daily: 3 mile jog at 6.45 am, swim after evening run.

Mon	am 7 miles easy, pm 6 miles steady (3.45 per km)
Tue	am 8 miles hilly fartlek, pm 6 miles steady plus 6 x 200m fast striding on the track
Wed	am 4 x 3 km at around 3.00 per km (5 min recovery), pm 6 miles easy
Thu	am 7 miles easy, pm 5 miles easy
Fri	am 10 miles at 3.30 per km, pm 5 miles easy plus 10 x 80m fast striding on track
Sat	am 10 x 1 km at 2.50 (2 min rest), pm 6 miles steady
Sun	Easy day, as Thursday (39km run the following day)

Week's total: 120-130 miles

The last part of the training really determines its own pattern, since one must have an easy week after returning from altitude. The three times a day training only continues for two weeks; after that the emphasis is on doing better quality sessions with longer recuperation periods, and the distance is reduced to 100-105 miles per week. A race can be fitted in immediately on returning or a week later, and the following weekend is needed for the last big (35-45km) run, approximately three weeks before the actual race. After that we start to taper, reducing the distance run in the last three weeks to roughly 80%, 60% and 40% of normal and only making a real effort on one or two days in each week. In the last week there are no serious efforts – this is the time for the race preparation described in Chapter 13.

After the marathon

When racing shorter distances, even the half-marathon, all you need for recovery is one or two easy days before getting on with training, but a marathon or an ultra-marathon has to be treated quite differently. The body suffers in several different ways, the most obvious being dehydration. Even on a cool day we lose a lot of water by sweating, and on a hot day a runner can lose four or five litres, or roughly a gallon, of sweat. Most runners are now aware of this danger and take drinks along the way, but if the runner does not drink enough, sweating may eventually stop. This is really dangerous, because the body temperature will then start to rise. At the finish of a hot weather marathon, some runners may have temperatures of up to 104 degrees Fahrenheit. The first thing to do in this situation is to bring the temperature down gradually, and the second is to replace the lost water.

The other problem which applies to races of twenty miles and over is that of

Richard Nerurkar in the European championships. The experienced runner carries his drink bottle for a long time.

26 miles or more on the road. Because the body is very good at making adjustments and shifting the strain from one part to another, injuries may not show up during the race but will appear in the next two weeks.

All these things reinforce the need for a prolonged rest after a marathon, with particular care needed in the first few hours.

exhaustion of the fuel supplies. Even if the athlete has not actually 'hit the wall', he is likely to have a low blood sugar and to have exhausted his glycogen stores. On top of that we have all the problems encountered by those whose joints and muscles are not up to running hard for

The post-race period will be much more pleasant if you have planned ahead. In a big-city race, it is often difficult to get away quickly for a shower, but you can wipe yourself down with a sponge and a towel and put on sweat-free clothes and clean socks. You should have a supporter or 'second' who will meet you at a pre-arranged spot and look after you on the way home. It will make your recovery much quicker if you do not set off on a long journey right after the race. Try to find somewhere where you can have a bath, a meal and a rest before travelling back.

In the first week after the marathon you should not force yourself to do any-thing. If you feel like running, keep it down to no more than a twenty-minute jog, but there is no harm in having a complete rest, or just walking to ease out the stiffness. A week after the race, you

Post-race routine

1. Lie down or sit down, in the shade if it is hot.
2. Cover with a sheet to prevent too much heat loss.
3. Sip a cool (not iced) sweet drink.
4. Use a sponge, sparingly, to bring the temperature down, sponging the forehead, back of the neck, wrists and back of the knees.
5. Eat something you enjoy – a banana, chocolate, energy bar.
6. Have a shower or bath.
7. Have a massage.

should start going out for a daily run, if you haven't already done so, but you should not try to run hard until you really feel like running. At the earliest, you should return to normal training two weeks after the race – but many people prefer to have a month of light exercise before thinking of anything else.

At the international level, few runners do more than three marathons a year and most will race seriously only twice a year over this distance, but these are the people who are pushing themselves right to the limit. 'Ultra' runners, on the other hand, will happily run a marathon once a month and just regard it as a long training run, because they are not pushing themselves to the limit.

It is a reasonable proposition for the 'serious amateur' to run two marathons with a gap of only six to eight weeks between them. This gives you the chance of getting two races from the one training period. The idea is to have two or three weeks' recovery, put in two weeks of normal training and then taper down to the next race. After that, you deserve a long time off.

Chapter 9

Beyond the marathon

For most runners, the marathon is the ultimate. I happen to think that this is the right attitude, for most people anyway. Human nature, however, is never satisfied. Our reach always exceeds our grasp. We always want to know what is over the horizon, beyond the next ridge. There is something fundamental, too, about ultimate endurance, as there is about ultimate speed. Children often ask me: 'What is the furthest distance you have run?' When I answer 'Three thousand miles', the next question is 'Did you stop at all?'

'Ultra' running means any event which is longer than a marathon, right up to trans-continental runs. For practical purposes we are mainly talking about runs over distances from 50 to 100 kilometres (30 to 62 miles) in length. The 100km distance is an established one, with international recognition and with championships held under IAAF rules, but the real attraction of ultra-running, like cross-country only more so, is that it is outside the bounds of formal competition (and for most of us, outside the bounds of human comprehension). Some races are on the road from point to point, like the Comrades Marathon and the London-to-Brighton run; others are over the mountains, like the Swiss Mountain Marathon;

and a few, very boringly in my opinion, are on the track, like the 24-hour run. Some achieve their 'ultra' status by being run as relays, like the Marathon des Sables, a French-organised event which involves five days of running through the deserts of North Africa. One of the events which captured the most worldwide interest was the Sydney-to-Melbourne race – just short of 1000 kilometres long (over 600 miles).

Everyone ought to try an ultra-run at least once in their career; it offers a whole new dimension to your running. If you are a miler and you run a marathon, you experience the same sort of thing – the lack of pressure, the freedom from a lung-bursting pace, the knowledge that you have plenty of time to get into a comfortable running rhythm. I only tried it once, when I ran from Los Angeles to New York in 1969, but I learned an awful lot during the year in which I prepared for it – and an awful lot more during the sixty-five days on the road!

Whether you are considering an ultra-race like the London-to-Brighton or the Comrades Marathon (both around 55 miles), a multi-day race like the Tour of Thameside or even perhaps a mega-event like the twenty-four hour run, the most important factor is durability. Speed becomes much less important, which opens the event up to all sorts of people who might not have considered themselves to be top-class runners. Another interesting aspect of ultra-running is that there is less difference in the performances of men and women, because although men are on average faster runners than women, they are equal in pure endurance. The longer the run, the more equal the contest.

I discovered in my own ultra-run that the only way to get really fit to run 350 miles a week is to run 350 miles a week, but fortunately that is neither desirable nor necessary for most ultra-events. The general principle holds good, though, that training is specific to the event. If you analyse the event and see what qualities are needed, those are the ones you have to work on. If you already possess some of them, so much the better.

Mental endurance is as important as physical endurance. If you are the kind of person who is thinking 'How much longer?' after fifteen minutes of a run, then ultras are not for you. If you can trot along for an hour and think 'this is fun' and then trot on for another couple of hours and think 'this is really fun', then you have found your event. The best way of building up this kind of strength is by doing long weekend 'rambles', part walking and part jogging, picking interesting countryside and thinking in terms of hours rather than miles. Once you are confident of spending four hours in continuous motion, you will be able to tackle your first ultra and find out whether you have a talent for it.

How much mileage is needed?

For most of us, training is limited by the time available, and so there is not much difference in the weekly and yearly mileage of the top marathon runners and the top ultra-runners. The bible of ultra-runners is *The Lore of Running* (Oxford University Press, 1984), by the South African doctor, Tim Noakes. Besides being very informative for marathon runners, the book is strongly slanted towards the Comrades Marathon, South Africa's greatest running event. The course between Durban and Pietermaritzburg is run alternately in the uphill and downhill directions (Durban being on the coast). The outstanding Comrades runner of the eighties was Bruce Fordyce, a man who would surely have been a star of the long-distance world had it not been for the boycotting of South African sport in his era. He set records for both the 'up' (5 hr 30 min) and the 'down' (5 hr 27 min) courses and has won the race more times than anyone else. In the five months leading up to the race his average monthly mileage was 360 and in the rest of the year he averaged less than 300 miles a month. It is interesting that after examining the career of many distance runners, Noakes comes to much the same conclusion as Arthur Lydiard, that about 100 miles a week, with a maximum of 120 miles, is enough for anyone. This is the maximum, but, as with the marathon, it is perfectly possible to run respectably and to enjoy the event on the basis of a much lower training mileage.

111

How many long training runs?

In other events, one runs the racing distance, or exceeds it, every day, but this is not advisable for ultras. I have run fifty miles a day for twenty days and all it does is make you very tired. The idea of one long run a week persists, except when there is a major race at the weekend, but this should not be enormously long every week. The marathon runner might go up to running 25-30 miles once a month in the last three months of training and the serious ultra-runner in the same time might do one run of 40 miles, two of 30 miles and the others of 18-26. The less serious ultra-runner would get most of his long-run experience from taking part in events, while his regular training would be the same as the average road-runner, with the addition of a long weekend run in the region of 15-20 miles.

How do I start?

The training you are able to do always depends on what you have been doing in the last month, so the first thing is to build yourself up gradually to the point where you are running at least five days a week and covering at least thirty miles a week. You will be running 5-6 miles on four days of the week and covering 8-10 miles on a Sunday, either in racing or training. If you want to follow a specific schedule, use one of the 10km programmes from Chapter 8 before moving onto the marathon

programme which suits your level. While keeping the weekday mileage the same, increase the weekend run from one hour to one-and-a-half hours for two weeks, then to two hours for two weeks. Having chosen your event, start tapering off eight days before by cutting your Sunday run back to one hour.

The last week before the race will look like this:

Sun	One hour easy
Mon	Rest
Tue	6 miles easy
Wed	5 miles brisk pace
Thu	4 miles easy
Fri	Rest
Sat	3 miles easy

Serious training

The following week's training is taken from an article by Don Ritchie in the Road Runners' Club publication *Training for Ultras*, edited by Andy Milroy.

Mon	8 miles
Tue	8.5 miles
Wed	am 14 miles to school, pm 14 miles back from school
Thu	am 14 miles to school, pm 8.5 back from school, then 8.5 hard run with club
Fri	am 14 miles to school, pm 12 miles back
Sat	No run. Felt tired
Sun	31 miles

It will be seen that the running is mostly at the same pace, and the total for the week was 130 miles. This was done just before Ritchie set a world best of 6 hr 10 min for 100km.

A typical week for Bruce Fordyce when training at his peak was:

Mon	am 5 miles, pm 10 miles
Tue	am 5 miles, pm 5 miles, interval or hill training
Wed	15 miles easy
Thu	am 5 miles, pm 6miles, hills or interval training
Fri	am 10 miles, pm 5 miles
Sat	am 5 miles, pm cross-country race
Sun	Long run, 26-40 miles

This gives a weekly total of 105-120 miles, with a considerable variety, and is in my view a better balanced programme than Don Ritchie's, and one less likely to result in a long-term build-up of fatigue.

Bruce Fordyce's basic principles of training, as quoted by Tim Noakes (*Lore of Running*, p. 201) are ones which every marathon coach will endorse. He gave the reasons for his success as:

1. Rarely doing too much
2. Leg strength from hill running
3. Extreme caution in training and racing – not losing his head
4. Having natural speed
5. Paying minute attention to details, to the point of paranoia
6. Using altitude training

Richard Nerurkar and I have used every one of those principles in devising his marathon training. What he calls 'rarely doing too much' may well include running 120 miles in some weeks, but that is well within the bounds of his capabilities.

Those who enjoy racing more than training will be encouraged by the fact that Cavin Woodward, one of the leading ultra-runners of the seventies and eighties, believed in racing every week, never ran more than 20 miles in a single training run and never did more than 75 miles, plus a race, in a single week.

Training for the JOGLE Run

Ever since the days of Billy Butlin's John o' Groats to Land's End walk, this route, about 870 miles (1400km) has been popular as a club relay event and every year a few people run it or walk it, usually as a charity fund-raising stunt. The record at present is just over 10 days, which means averaging over eighty miles (120km) per day.

I have never done this run, but since my cross-America jaunt I have often been asked for advice about it, and the same general principles apply.

1. Establish a 'plateau' of training of 100 miles a week for ten weeks leading up to the event.
2. Start by doing one 'ultra' day a week, e.g. 40-50 miles. Each day should be split into 4 outings of 8-18 miles.

3. Progress to doing weekends of two or three 'ultra-days' in succession, e.g. 90-100 miles in two days, or 130-150 miles in 3 days. This gives you a chance to practice the 'running-eating-resting-running' routines.

4. After each ultra-session, cut your daily running to 30 minutes a day until you feel recovered.

5. Taper off your running in the last two weeks before the event. Reduce the mileage to half the normal distance two weeks before and a quarter of the normal distance in the last week.

Eating and drinking

Keeping up your fuel supply and avoiding dehydration are two of the most important factors in delaying tiredness. Carbo-loading will help, but between two and three days is the time needed to bring the stores up to their maximum, and the stores will be depleted in the first few hours of running unless you refuel constantly. Here is where the new carbohydrate drinks and power bars come into their own, because they are easily portable and full of energy, but there is a lot to be said for cups of tea, Mars bars and jam butties, because they taste good. The more tired you get, the more important it is to have something palatable. When I ran across America I was taking drinks every half hour and eating every four hours.

If I were attempting the JOGLE myself, aiming at, say, forty miles a day, I would structure my day like this:

7 am	Cup of tea and slice of bread and honey. Walk-jog 6 miles in just under an hour.
8.15-9.15 am	Large breakfast.
10.00-11.30 am	Run 10 miles.
12.00 noon	Lunch, mainly bread, soup, salad
2.15-3.45 pm	Run 10 miles

If you are just aiming to finish, take your time and drink thoroughly.

4.00-4.30 pm	Tea, bread and honey, banana, energy bar.
5.00-6.30 pm	Run 10 miles
7.00-8.00 pm	Supper – mainly pasta or rice dish
8.15-9.15 pm	Walk 4 miles in an hour
10.00 pm	Cocoa and biscuits

This assumes that one has long summer days and a support vehicle. It also allows time for washing the feet and sponging the legs after each stage. The essential principle is that one breaks the running down into manageable sections and gets plenty of food and drink after each stage.

Rest

This is an essential part of your training. Unless you can get proper rest after the effort, you will just get more tired. Try to organize things so that you can get a shower and some food after each session, and daily massage too, if possible. Have recuperation days built into your training programme and structure it into segments of, say, 7, 10 or 14 days. At the beginning of each segment you should be fresh and ready for the next – if not, give yourself another rest day.

Tapering

If you are training along the lines of a marathon schedule, but putting in longer weekend runs, the temptation is to try to get in just one more big week or one more big run. Avoid it. If in doubt, cut down. If

your regular mileage is 100-120 per week, then your last four weeks before the event should be:

Weeks to go	Distance
4	100 miles
3	90
2	60
1	20

It is only with proper tapering that you will be really ready for the big event. It is tempting to do more, but believe me, it will do more harm than good. The body needs time to repair the damage, build up fuel stores and generally get strong for the race.

The Race

Always remember that you are running against the course far more than against other people. The comradeship amongst ultra-runners is evidence of this. You are more likely to get the best out of yourself if you approach the race in a supportive, 'all in the same boat' frame of mind. It may happen that at the end of the hundred kilometres or the Comrades Marathon you still have another competitor alongside you, but this really only matters if you are in contention for the top three places. You just go out there and do what you can do. It may become competitive in the last five miles, but it is usually a matter of who has the most strength left, so tactics hardly come into it. The essential thing is knowing what you are capable of, so that you can choose the right pace from the start and run the race which suits you best.

The key to success in long races is staying in equilibrium, being in control, 'keeping your head together'. This requires planning, in terms of food and drink, and it requires close monitoring of your condition, so that you can ease off or take a drink *before* you get into dehydration or deep exhaustion rather than when it is too late. It will help a great deal if you have someone to support you who knows what you need, so that the drink is there just when you need it.

You must know the course and know what to expect in terms of weather. You will be in no fit state after four hours of running to cope with an unexpected thousand-foot climb and if you are not dressed for cold wind and rain on top of a mountain you can be completely wiped out by it.

Finally, never be inhibited from stopping and walking when you think you need to. A few minutes of walking and taking some food can make all the difference between covering the last ten miles in good heart, as opposed to turning into a shambling wreck. It is the end result which matters, not your image – and if you can cope with events of this length you won't have to worry about your image anyway.

Post-race

The remarks made in Chapter 8 all apply here, only more forcibly, because the totally exhausted ultra-runner can come close to death and there are, very occasionally, deaths caused either by over-heating or by a combination of hypothermia and under-nourishment. Taking care of the runners after the race is usually the concern of the race organizer, but each runner must give thought beforehand about how he is going to recover after the event. Have your favourite foods and drinks ready at the end. Have fresh clothing to change back into. If no showers are available; try to make your own arrangements for shower, rest and massage as soon as possible; and don't set yourself anything stressful to do right after the race – the journey back should be as comfortable as possible and the next few days should be as easy, physically, as you and your friends can make them. You may say 'never again', but the odds are that you'll be back next year, so take care of yourself.

Cross-country

What is the toughest race in the world? Some would say the Olympic marathon, some the Western States 100-miler, others the Hawaiian Iron Man. I would suggest that the hardest one to win is the World Cross-Country Championships. This is the only race in which you will find the World and Olympic champions at 5000 metres, 10,000 metres and steeplechase lined up against the top road runners, the winners of the New York and Boston marathons, the holders of European, Commonwealth and Olympic medals. Of all these champions, only one can be the race winner on that day. There are no mile markers, no even laps to be reeled off, no pacemaker to do the hard work and then step aside. It is twelve kilometres of uninhibited running, starting with a blistering first half-mile and scarcely letting up for the rest of the way. It is a great leveller. World-class runners can be left floundering by lesser-known men. Reputations are worthless. Nothing counts except how fit and fast you are on that day, in that weather, over that course.

If you have started your running on the road, you may never have come across the delights of cross-country running. Its principal attraction lies in its contrast with the track and road versions of the sport. The only feature they share is having a start and a finish – apart from that, cross-country lacks all the things which make performances quantifiable. The surfaces are uneven and widely varied even in the course of a single race. The distances are seldom precisely measured and even if they were, the changes in surface and slope make time comparisons meaningless.

The breaks in continuity prevent the runners from getting into a rhythm, the heavy and uneven going demands a different style as well as more leg strength, and the runners may also have to contend with fences, ditches, dogs and cattle. Physically, it is tough, but, perhaps for that very reason, it is much more fun than track or road. Wherever you finish in the field, there is satisfaction in having braved the elements and completed the course. Perhaps there is some deeply buried folk-memory of our days as hunting animals which derives satisfaction from proving ourselves in a natural setting.

Most cross-country runners, however, do not engage in the sport for the sake of therapy. They do it partly because it is the ideal way for a distance runner to build up aerobic fitness and physical toughness, and partly because it is a highly competitive sport in its own right, with its frameworks of competition leading from the smallest club and school to those mind-blowing world championship races.

Cross-country differs enormously from country to country. In hot, dry countries such as South Africa, Kenya and the West of America, you will be running on hard ground, wearing road shoes or rubber studs, but on a 'traditional' British, Irish or Belgian course you may be up to your ankles in mud and wearing long spikes, and in a championship race, where the numbers are large, you will be running on open grassland – park or playing field. Some courses include stretches of road, which makes the choice of footwear difficult.

The distances are pretty standard – generally 5-6 miles (8-10km) for men, 3-4 miles (5-6.4 km) for women. The courses may be made up of one large lap, which means that the runners disappear from sight and only re-appear twenty or thirty minutes later, or they may be of several laps. The typical European course has a lap of about 1500 metres, which includes a soccer field or a stadium. This makes the course much more suitable for spectators and more easily shown on television, so there is more sponsorship and more razzamatazz. At the highest level, the Grand

Prix series of cross-countries in Europe, it is a professional sport, with the best men and women earning a few thousand dollars every time they race. By contrast, an inter-club league race in the West of England will have virtually no spectators except the club officials and a few loyal husbands, wives and parents. There are no prizes and everyone pays his own way, but the commitment to the race and the feeling of satisfaction afterwards is no less great.

Physically, the benefits of cross-country are the same for all. Both the training and the competition are excellent for all-round conditioning. Since they involve at least twenty and sometimes forty minutes of continuous running, the aerobic systems are fully stretched. Running uphill has some of the same effects on the legs as weight training, because you are pushing your own body weight up the hills. Running over uneven going makes demands on the ankles in particular. The runner who can cope with a tough cross-country course is a more robust runner than one who is used only to flat smooth surfaces, hence the good track runner who uses cross-country as part of his build-up will be an even better track runner when the next season comes round.

Cross-country events in summer can present a heat problem - so be prepared

There will always be some runners who are physically better suited to cross-country than any of the other disciplines, because of their build or their running style. The best track runners tend to run more on their toes and rely on perfect balance to make them efficient movers at high speeds. If their mechanical efficiency is spoilt by slippery or rough ground, then they can be beaten by somebody whose style can cope with it. For this alone, cross-country has its place, because it gives more runners a chance of achieving something worthwhile. A classic example is John Ngugi, the outstanding cross-country runner of his day, five times world champion. He did succeed on one big occasion on the track, winning the 1988 Olympic 5000 metres, but he never achieved the awesome dominance he showed over the country, where he could demolish everybody, whether it was a fast grass course, heavy mud or, on the last occasion, Boston 1992, snow-covered heather.

Cross-country training

Typically, the cross-country season operates at a time when there is not much track running going on, therefore cross-country training acts as the endurance training for middle and long-distance track runners. It has a lot to recommend it for marathon runners, too. Steve Moneghetti and Richard Nerurkar have regularly used cross-country to provide a break from a year-round road season.

However, no one must forget that to

Dry conditions favour the runner who has natural speed.

perform well on any surface you have got to run fast, so cross-country training is by no means all plodding. I think of it as ten-thousand metres training on soft going. The best training involves running a good bit faster than the anaerobic threshold level. The main components will be:

Short hills – for leg power

Long hills – leg power plus cardiovascular fitness

Cross-country reps – cardiovascular and speed-endurance training

Fast aerobic runs – cardiovascular training

Fartlek – provides a bit of everything

Long slow runs – general endurance plus recuperation

Short slow runs – recuperation only

Weights and circuit training – all round body strength

The period of training

After a track or road season, there should be a time when the athlete takes a break. In Europe and North America, the early autumn is the best time for slow endurance runs, which develop into cross-country training as the autumn progresses. Although the American cross-country season virtually finishes in November, the European season does not reach its peak until the World Championships in March. However, there are some quite big races before Christmas, including the newly established European Championships. This structure is paralleled in the school and collegiate systems, so that the runner may find him or herself competing right through from October onwards.

It is advisable to have no more than four months of doing the same kind of training – very often three is enough – followed by a racing period. I therefore advise dividing the six months from 1 October to 31 March into at least two blocks, with distinct goals in each time-span. A road-runner might decide to compete on the road until the end of October, take November as a break and then to concentrate on cross-country from December until early March, by which time he will be moving back into road training for the April season.

A track runner could follow the American pattern – a short cross-country season, followed by indoor track running in January and February – or he could have a long autumn break and then start in December to build up to a full cross-country season, going through to March. What I do *not* recommend is finishing the track season on 1 September, starting the endurance build-up on 2 September and moving on to full cross-country fitness by mid-October. By December the runner has nowhere further to go and he or she will find it very difficult to remain at full racing fitness through to championship time in March. One way round it would be to have a racing period in November/December and a 'hibernation period' over Christmas. Another would be to go away in the winter for some altitude or warm-weather training before building up again to another racing period.

Training volume

The middle-distance track runner will probably be doing his highest mileage during the winter months and the 5km/10km runner will be running as much in the winter as in the hardest part of spring training. The marathon runner might be doing slightly less when he in his cross-country training phase, because he is not doing his long runs so often. As with any hard training period, you must build up gradually from what was being done before, and the move from steady running to hard sessions should not be done in a single jump, but by bringing in first one hard session a week and then two.

Under-20 cross-country runner

Mon Repetition runs, e.g. 4 x 1200m on grass (4 min rest)

Tue 6 miles Fartlek, with many short bursts

Wed Hill training, e.g. 8 x 300m uphill, jog back

Thu 6-7 miles on road, starting slowly, with a fast 4-mile, stretch in the middle, last mile easy

Variations on the theme

You should have at least one alternative session for each one listed above. For the hills you need something short and steep which takes only 15-20 seconds to run up, and you might have a really long hill which you do only occasionally, say a 2 x 1000m session. You should have two or three different repetition courses. Some of these will have to be on the road under street lights so that you can do them on wet winter evenings, and the distances can be from 1100m up to over 2000m. The routes you use for your road runs should be varied too. If you train with a club on one or two nights a week, or go to a friend's house and run from there, it will prevent you from repeating yourself too much. If you have two alternatives for each session given above, then you can do three weeks which are all different and start again, or else have a low mileage week followed by a race before starting another four-week block.

Additions

Most clubs will have some kind of weight or circuit training in the winter and this is something I would recommend for the young runner. To make progress you should be doing this twice a week. You should not omit a running session for an indoor session, unless the weather makes it dangerous to run, but you can make the run easier if the weights session has been hard. For example, the Thursday and Sunday runs could just be a little more comfortable, giving your body a chance to absorb the benefit of the strength training. See Appendices C and D for Circuit and Weight Training.

There is little in here that relates to the track training most people will be doing after the cross-country season. You should include a session of fast striding on a good surface twice a week, either as part of your warm-up or on the end of a steady run. The distance can be anything between 100 and 200m – 6 x 150m would be alright. and the pace should build up from an easy stride to something just below flat out sprinting, so that you are using a long stride with plenty of knee-lift. In Peter Coe's words: 'The runner should never be too far away from speed'.

Fri	Rest		**Tue**	Repetition session, 4-5 x 1 mile, 3 min rests
Sat	Warm-up, race, cool-down		**Wed**	6-8 miles easy pace
Sun	Long, slow run, 10-12 miles, or 'split' session, 5 + 5		**Thu**	Hill or interval session, plus warm-up and cool-down

Week's total: 40-48 miles a week

Club cross-country runner

This is for the adult runner who is prepared to put in fifty miles a week – enough to perform well at the level of county championships, inter-school and inter-club events. If you hope to do well at regional and national level, where you have to race over nine miles, you will have to move, eventually, up to the next schedule.

Read the general principles set out in the under-20 schedule – they apply just as much to you.

Week 1 (Sunday league race)

Mon	7-8 miles Fartlek, starting easy, then putting in bursts

Tue	Repetition session, 4-5 x 1 mile, 3 min rests
Wed	6-8 miles easy pace
Thu	Hill or interval session, plus warm-up and cool-down
Fri	5 miles, mostly easy, plus strides, 8 x 150m
Sat	Rest
Sun	Warm-up, race, cool-down, 10 miles total

Week's total: 48 miles approx.

Week 2 (Saturday race)

Mon	8 miles easy
Tue	Repetition session, 6 x 1000m, 2 min recovery
Wed	8 miles Fartlek
Thu	5 miles steady plus 8 x 200m stride or 10 x 400m hills if Saturday's race is not major
Fri	Rest
Sat	Warm-up, race, cool-down, 10 miles total

Wet conditions sort out the 'real' cross-country men from the boys.

Sun   10-14 miles slow and easy, or 'split' session, 7+5

Week's total: 52 miles approx.

Variations on the theme

Over the preparation period before racing starts, which may be 4-6 weeks, the weekends allow for a high mileage. Sometimes you may be at a training camp, putting in five sessions over the Friday-Sunday period. If you are doing two sessions a day, one will probably be recuperation or just and endurance run and the other will contain some hard work. The 'split' session mentioned allows one to do a slow recuperation run in the morning and then something a bit faster in the afternoon, possibly including some fast stride-outs over 200-300 metres.

During the main part of the training, when you may be racing but you are not cutting right down before big races, you should try to make the programme progressive. This means gradually increasing the number of hill runs or intervals you are doing. The hills should be as indicated in the under-20 schedule. The intervals can be on any surface. University runners, for example, may be able to get onto a track and do 10 x 400 early in the year, increasing to 16 x 400m later on, or they may have a set session of 8 x 800 metres where the average time gets a bit faster every two or three weeks.

National level cross-country runner

This athlete has already had at least four years of consistent training and so has the physical and mental capacity to absorb 80 miles a week. This volume is normal for male runners, who may even go up to 100 miles a week, and it is done by the best female runners – which is perhaps the reason that they are the best.

The increase in volume is mainly achieved by putting in an extra run on Mondays to Fridays, but the long weekend run is usually longer and the amount of hard work, hill climbs or repetitions, slightly more than that for the club level. Because the athlete at national level is that much fitter, the speed will be slightly faster and the recovery times slightly shorter.

Week 1 (Minor race)

Mon-Fri: am 5-6 miles steady. Second session as shown

Mon	8-10 miles steady pace, plus strides at the end
Tue	8-10 miles Fartlek, doing 2 min fast, 2min slow
Wed	8 x 800m up long hill, jogging back
Thu	6 miles easy
Fri	am session only
Sat	Warm-up and race, followed by 5 miles warm-down
Sun	15 miles continuous run

Week's total: 80-85 miles

123

Week 2 (Major race on Sunday)

Mon-Fri: am 5-6 miles steady, pm session as shown

Mon	Warm-up, 4 x 2000m reps, 5 min rest
Tue	10 miles at good pace
Wed	12 x 400m hills
Thu	5 miles easy, plus 8 x 200m strides
Fri	am session only
Sat	Travelling, plus 5 miles easy
Sun	Warm-up, race, 3 miles cool-down.

Week's total: 75 miles approx

Variations on the theme

In the pre-racing period, there is the opportunity for an additional hard session at the weekend, instead of a race. A suitable race-related session is to do, after a warm-up, 15 minutes hard, then 10 minutes hard, then 5 minutes hard, each followed by a five-minute recovery jog. Both the going and the kind of shoes you wear should be similar to that of a race.

Catherine McKiernan (Ireland) wins the first European Cross-Country championship race for women.

Cross-country racing tactics

See Chapter 13 for details of this.

Track running

If you ask a member of the general public to name an athlete, they will generally give the name of a track athlete. In Britain, in the nineties, the name you are most likely to get is 'Linford Christie'.

If you had asked that question in the eighties, the response might have been 'Seb Coe', 'Steve Ovett' or 'Steve Cram', all of whom, like Linford, had been either World or Olympic champions. A generation ago the reply might have been 'Brendan Foster' or 'Dave Bedford'. In every generation there are heroes and heroines of the track and they serve as role models for the next generation, which in turn will produce its own stars. When I was a teenager I was inspired by the running of the great Emil Zatopek, who won three gold medals in the 1952 Olympics. There is something pure and straightforward about racing on the track. We can identify with it and we can appreciate what the runners are going through. Seeing them overcome their pain and produce a great finish touches a chord in everyone.

Track running is part of track and field athletics, whose growth has been closely linked to the growth of the modern Olympic movement. With a few minor exceptions, the track events in a standard athletics meeting include most of those in the Olympic programme. The standard Olympic track events for men are 100m, 200m, 400m, 800m, 1500m, 5000m,

10,000m, 110m hurdles, 400m hurdles, 3000m steeplechase and the two relays, the 4 x 100m and 4 x 400m. The women's programme is now the same except for the lack of a steeplechase. The 10,000m is seldom run in club events, and quite often the 5000m is replaced by a 3000m, which until recently was an Olympic event for women.

Because track running needs a track, an expensive item to construct, the number of proper track and field athletics clubs is less than that of road running clubs – another factor which tends to make it more elitist – but track running is still a very cheap sport compared to, say, tennis or golf, and it is accessible to anyone living in a city or large town which is prepared to make the effort to get to a track. At the lower end it is a poor man's sport, but at the peak of the pyramid track runners are amongst the world's most admired athletes, able to command fees of thousand of dollars for a single race. Track athletes are the thoroughbreds of the human racing world.

Track running is essentially about speed, even when one is dealing with the longer distances. The opportunity of races for people of all abilities, which we see in road running, cannot apply to the track, because there is simply not enough room. On the road, it is not unusual for the tail-enders in a race to take more than twice the time of the winner, but this situation would cause chaos on the track. In normal club competition, each club enters its best two runners in each event and in championship events there are qualifying times for entry. However, there are opportunities for the newcomer or the less talented athlete at the lower levels. District and County championships generally have no entry restrictions, and there are also 'graded meetings' where anyone can enter and the entries are divided into races, twenty or so per race, based on ability.

If you are keen to develop your potential and learn all you can about the sport, you must use track running as part of your development. It is on the track that speed is developed, because the opportunities to run 5000 and 10,000 metres are limited and most distance runners find themselves running the 800 and 1500 metres. This means that if you are going to achieve anything, you have to be running your 400m laps in about one minute – a little less for male 800m runners and a little more for female 1500m runners. A good mile time for a young man might be 4 min 10 sec (equivalent to 3 min 52 for 1500m), which means lapping in about 62 seconds. Contrast this with the world of the road runner, where a good man might be running at five minutes per mile (75 seconds a lap) and the majority of runners in a race are running at slower than six minute miles (90 seconds a lap). This has got nothing to do with the shoes or the surface – it is just that those good enough to compete on the track have to match up to a high standard; there is no room for slow

runners, so it's a case of 'shape up or ship out'. Having said that, track running responds to training just as much as any other branch of the sport and the nice thing about it is that you know exactly where you are. You can't fool anybody, but if you can run the times you will get your chance.

Sprinting and hurdling

Because this book deals with distance running, these events fall outside my compass and it would be doing nobody a favour to treat them in an oversimplified way. If you want to develop in that direction, get in touch with your local athletic club and find a coach.

Sprinting speed is needed by all track runners.

Middle-distance running

This covers the distances from 800 metres to 1500 metres, which are usually the longest distances run in school competition. Hence, even though your talents may eventually lie in the 10,000 metres or the marathon, it is likely that you will start here. Because they are races with a large aerobic component, runners need to have a background of general endurance running before they start. In most cases, those who start training for a summer season will have had a background of running road or cross-country during the winter. They will therefore be fit enough to start one of these programmes.

What makes these distances so fascinating, though, is the fact that there is also a large anaerobic factor, or, to put it another way, speed is very important. To be a top-class 1500m runner you must also be a very good 800m runner, which means that you must also be pretty good at 400m. The middle-distance runner must be able to run efficiently at a variety of paces and must be able to change smoothly from one pace to another. He will usually have an equal mixture of 'fast-twitch ' and 'slow-twitch' fibres in his muscles (see Chapter 3) and his training may be slanted more in the direction of endurance or more in the direction of speed, depending on which one he needs most.

Long-distance running

This means the 5000m and the 10,000m and the steeplechase for adult runners,

A top-class marathon runner must also be good on the track.

and includes the 3000m for younger runners. The anaerobic component in these races is much less, so they will attract the kind of people who do well in cross-country and road running, people with more 'slow-twitch' fibres and less basic speed. However, the competition at the highest level demands the ability to run the last 400m in under 55 seconds in men's races and around 60 seconds in women's races, so speed training must not be ignored.

Using spikes

Spiked shoes help you to run faster, but you must learn to use them properly.

Spike size
- 5-6 mm. Suitable for the synthetic, rubberised, 'tartan' track surfaces which are found on most modern tracks and on the run-ups for High, Long and Triple Jump and Pole Vault. Spikes longer than 6mm must not be used on these surfaces.
- 9 mm. Suitable for cinder tracks, clay tracks and 'Redgra' surfaces. The best length for most cross-country courses.
- 12 mm. Suitable for running on grass except when very wet or very dry.
- 15 mm. Used for cross-country or for grass tracks, when very soft.

Running action. Spikes only help you if you are running on your toes for part or all of the time. The faster you run, the more help they will be, because they prevent you from slipping when your toes push against the ground. However, getting up on your toes like this does put a lot of extra strain on your calf muscles and Achilles tendon.

When you first use spikes, warm up in your trainers beforehand, and then do some strides in your spikes. Use them for a small part of the session and finish off the rest in flat shoes. You will probably feel a little stiff in the calves the next day and you should stick to easy running until this wears off. The next time you have a track session, do half of it in spikes and half in flats. After three or four sessions in spikes your muscles should become adjusted to them, but your warm-up and cool-down periods should be longer than when running in trainers.

Basic principles

You have to get your body and mind adjusted to the speed or rhythm of your racing distance and you have to be fit enough to handle that speed for the duration of the event. More than anything else, track training is about speed-endurance. If you want to run a mile in 4.10, you have to get used to maintaining the 62-second lap speed. The classic way to train for this is by interval training. You might start with a lap speed that feels fast but not impossibly so – say 67 seconds a lap. You run one lap at this speed, jog slowly until you have got your breath back and then do the same again. In an early session you might run eight fast laps, with a recovery time of between two and three minutes and an average time of 67.4 seconds. This goes down in your training log as '8 x 400m, 67.4 (2-3 min)'. A week later you might repeat the session and find that you can average

67.0, keeping your recovery time down to exactly 2 minutes. As you get fitter your average time will gradually come down and you will be able to do more of them. The number of possible variations is limitless, because you can vary the speed, the number of runs and the length of the recovery time. I would recommend fixing the volume of the session and the recovery time, at least for a month, and work on the speed. Later, you might re-assess yourself and decide that you could handle more, with a shorter recovery.

However, the development of aerobic ability is equally important, and so the middle-distance runner must keep his aerobic fitness training going throughout the track season. This is done by repetition runs, hill runs and by steady runs at slower than threshold pace. Speed work needs to be done, too, and so does mobility training. The art of track training lies in combining all these elements without overloading the athlete. As fitness develops, so he is able to cope with more and harder training. Even with an adult athlete it may take five years to reach full potential and starting at the age of 14 it is likely to take ten years – so both coach and athlete have to be patient.

The programmes below cannot possibly cover all sorts and conditions of runner, but from the six different ability levels it should be possible for everyone to adapt one of them to his own use.

Lap speed

'1500m tempo' means the pace at which you could run 1500m, in ideal conditions, at the time of the training. Thus, somebody who ran 4 min 40 last year and is hoping to run under 4 min 30 will start his sessions at 4 min 40 pace (75 sec a lap, approx).

To find your correct lap speed, convert the intended 1500m time into seconds, divide it by 15 to get the pace per 100m and then multiply by 4. A 4 min 40 1500m is 280 seconds, divided by 15 is 18.67, multiplied by 4 = 74.7 seconds per lap.

Track schedule 1

17-year-old boy. Target times for 1500m: 4 min 20; for 800m: 2.06

17-year-old girl. Target times for 1500m: 4 min 45; for 800m: 2.18

Lap times:
1500m: 69/70 sec (M), 75/76 sec (W);
800m: 63 sec(M), 69 sec (W)

Weekly pattern

Mon	Endurance work, either on flat grass or hills
Tue	Track session, 1500m tempo
Wed	30-45 min easy running
Thu	Track session, 800m tempo
Fri	Rest or easy jog

Sat   Minor race or time trial

Sun   Long slow run, one hour approx, plus strides

As the athlete moves from the build-up phase to the pre-competition phase, he will bring in first one and then two or three track sessions a week, while maintaining a basis of steady runs. The last six weeks of training before competition starts should include the items listed in each week.

Week 1

Endurance:	6 x 600m on grass (2 min jog recovery)
1500m session:	2 x (4 x 400m) with 200m jog recovery and 400m jog after first set. Aim at 71 sec for first set, 69 sec for second set
800m session:	6 x 300m, in 47-48 sec, with 3-4 min rest
Distance:	Two steady runs of 5-7 miles each

Week 2

Endurance:	Hill training, 10 x 60 sec uphill
1500m session:	Pyramid session(200-400 600-800-600 00-200) at 70 72 400m pace, with 200m jog for each 400m fast
800m session:	2 x (8 x 200m) at 30-31 sec each, 200m jog
Distance:	Two runs, 6-8 miles

Week 3

Endurance:	3 x 800 approx, plus 3 x 600 approx, with equal time recovery, on grass
1500m session:	2 x (5 x 400m), as Week 1, but aim at 70 sec average in first set and 68 sec average in the second. Recovery jog 200m after each one, extra 200m after the first set
800m session:	6 x 300m as Week 1, but aim at 46-47 sec
Distance:	Two runs of 5-8 miles each

Week 4

Endurance:	Hill session as Week 2, but faster
1500m session:	Pyramid (400-600-800-800-600-400) at 70, 71 pace per 400m, recoveries as in Week 2.
800m session:	4 x 400m in 60-62 sec, with 5 min rest
Distance:	Two runs of 5-8 miles

Week 5

Endurance:	6 x 600m (as Week 3) + 2 x 300m, faster pace
1500m session:	4 x 400m, 68-69 sec, 2 min recovery, then 4 x 300m in 49-50 sec with 90 sec recovery
800m session:	4 x 300m and 4-6 x 200m, at 800m pace
Distance:	One 6-mile run

Competition:	Minor race or 2 x 3 min hard on grass, with a 6 min rest between the two.

Week 6

Endurance:	None
1500m session:	3 sets of (4 x 400m) at 72,70,68 pace, with a 200m jog in 90 sec, plus extra 2 min after each set
800m session:	2 sets of 8 x 200m, untimed, around race pace
Distance run:	One 6-mile run
Competition:	1500m race

Track schedule 2

Club level 800/1500m runner. Target times for 1500m: 3 min 58 (men) 4 min 25 (women); for 800m 2 min 0 (men) 2 min 12 (women)

1500m speed is 64 sec (M), 70 sec (W)
800m speed is 60 sec (M), 66 sec (W)

This follows the same principles as Schedule 1, in assuming that the runner already has a good background of endurance and aerobic training. Endurance is maintained by the regular long run and by keeping the weekly mileage in the region of 40-50 miles (60-80km) per week. Each week's training should include the elements shown, with the hard session interspersed with steady runs of 5-8 miles. The times shown are for men, but the appropriate women's times can be substituted with no other change. Each week will contain a combination of repetition sessions, interval training and speed sessions, plus at least one endurance day.

Week 1

Endurance:	10 miles
Repetition:	6 x 1000m, off the track, 2 min recovery
Intervals:	8 x 600, slower than 1500 pace, 2 min recovery

Sonia O'Sullivan (Ireland), the world 5000m champion, leads Paula Radcliffe in a Grand Prix race.

Speed:	Sprint drills + 30 min fartlek, with short bursts

Week 2

Endurance:	8 miles
Repetition:	4 x 1200m, off the track, 2-3 min recovery
Intervals:	12 x 400m at 1500m pace, 90 sec recovery
Speed:	2 sets of 8 x 200m, untimed, 60 sec recovery, plus sprint drills

Week 3

Endurance:	10 miles
Repetition:	6 x 800m, off the track, 2 min recovery
Intervals:	3 x (4 x 400m) at 68, 66, 64, 90 sec jog between runs 3 min jog between sets
Speed:	Sprint drills plus 10 x 120m fast on grass

Week 4

Endurance:	8 miles
Intervals:	8 x 600m at 1500m pace, 400m jog recovery
Speed:	4 x 200m, 2 x 400m, 4 x 200m, at 800m pace, with 2 min recovery after 200m, 4 min after 400m

Week 5

Endurance:	8 miles or 'split', am 6 miles, pm 4 miles
Intervals:	10 x 400m in 64-65, 90 sec recovery jog

Speed:	6 x 300m at 800m speed, 3 min recovery

Week 6

Endurance:	8 miles or 5+ 5 split session
Repetition:	4 x 1000m off the track, 2 min recovery
Intervals:	3 x (4 x 400m), as Week 3, but faster
Speed:	Race over 800m or 200, 300, 400, 500, 200, all fast, with 1 min recovery for every 100m run.

Track schedule 3

National level 1500m runner. Target times for 1500m: 3 min 40(men), 4 min 14 (women); for 800m: 1 min 49 (men) 2 min 6 (women)

Lap times: 1500m 58-60 (men), 66-68 (women); 800m 54-55 (men), 63 sec (women)

The principles of transferring from a base of good aerobic training to running two or more hard track sessions a week must be done gradually, along the lines given in the two schedules above. However, to reach this level the training has to be more complex, in order to cover all the aspects the top-class middle-distance runner needs. This is what I call the 'Coe' cycle, because it is based on the multipace system used so successfully by the double Olympic champion. This is described in detail in the book by

The steeplechase needs the stamina of a 5000m runner and the speed of a 1500m runner – as well as technique.

Peter Coe and David Martin, *Training Distance Runners* (Human Kinetics Publishers, 1991).

In a two-week cycle the athlete does hard sessions at five different paces. These are interspersed with recuperation runs and endurance runs, with the total mileage being in the region of 50-60 miles (80-96km) per week in the pre-competition period.

A sessions – 5000m pace: 4-5 x 1200m or 5-6 x 1000m or pyramid session of 800-1000-1200-1000-800-400. Recovery time not longer than 1 min per 400m run.

B sessions – 3000m pace: 6 x 800 or 8 x 600

C sessions – 1500m pace: 10 x 400m, 75-90 sec recovery or 3 x (4 x 400m), with 75sec recovery and 3 min after each set

D sessions – 800m pace: 6 x 300m or 4 x 400m or pyramid session of 200, 300 ,400, 500, 200, with 1 min recovery for every 100m run.

E sessions – 400m pace: 2 x (300-200-150),with 4-5 min after each fast run

Two-week cycle

Sun	Endurance run, 10-12 miles
Mon	Fartlek on grass, plus sprint drills
Tue	A session
Wed	Steady run, 6-8 miles
Thu	B session
Fri	Rest or 25 min easy jog
Sat	D session
Sun	8 miles easy run
Mon	C session (E when closer to competition)
Tue	Easy run, 6 miles
Wed	C or D session, reduced volume before serious race
Thu	Easy running for 30 min plus strides
Fri	Rest or 20 min jog
Sat	Race or 2 x 5 min hard on grass (10 min recovery)

Track schedule 4

Club level 5000/3000m runner. Target times 15.00/8.45 (men) 16.40/sub-10.00 (women)

133

3000m pace is 70 a lap (men), 78 a lap (women)
5000m pace is 72 a lap (men), 80 a lap (women)

The basic pattern here entails three days of hard training a week in a non-racing week, interspersed with one rest day and two steady runs, the seventh day being an endurance run. In weeks where there is a race or a time trial at the end of the week, the hard sessions are done on Monday and Wednesday, allowing for two or three days of tapering. To cover the full spectrum, the runner should have one session a week which is larger in volume but slower in tempo than his race, and one session a week where the tempo is faster and the volume shorter. The pattern for a two-week period would look like this:

Mon	6 miles easy plus 6 x 150m fast stride
Tue	4 x 1200 or 5 x 1000m, at 5000m pace, 3-4 min recovery
Wed	6 miles brisk run
Thu	4 x (800 + 400), with 200 jog recovery, 3000 m pace
Fri	Rest
Sat	3 x (4 x 400m) at 1500m pace, 60 sec recovery
Sun	8-10 miles easy
Mon	3 x 2400m, off the track, at 10km race pace, 5 min recovery
Tue	6-7 miles steady
Wed	2 x (8 x 200m) at 1500m pace, 60 sec recovery
Thu	4 miles easy run
Fri	Rest or 20 min jog
Sat	Race or 10 min hard, 5 min hard, 2 min hard, off the track (5 min jog recovery after each)
Sun	10 miles steady run

Track schedule 5

National level 5000m runner. Target times sub 14.00 min (men), sub 15.30 (women)

Two week cycle, based on microcycles of 3 days. Within each micro cycle, one day is hard, the following easy and the next moderately hard, followed by another hard day. In a non-racing period, a week will be made up of two 3-day microcycles plus a long run of 75-90 minutes. In a racing week, the last hard training is done on the Tuesday or Wednesday, followed by 2 x (8 x 200m) on Wed or Thurs, and a tapering period (see Chapter 13).

Main training sessions

Moderate	
M1	2 miles of warming up, then 3-5 miles good aerobic pace
M2	after warm-up, brisk runs of 15 min, 10 min, 5 min, with 3-5 min slow jog between each
M3	(For wet days) 6 x (50 double strides, 60 sec jog 100 double strides)
M4	13 x 1 minute at 80% effort on grass or slight hill

Hard

H1	1000m-2000m-2000m-1000m all at 69-67, plus 2 x 200 fast 3 min rest after 1000, 5 min after 2000.
H2	4 x (1000 + 400), with 1000 at 67-68, 30 sec jog, 400 in 64, then 300m walk jog (2 min)
H3	1000-600-400 (68-66-64 pace)
H4	2 x 8 x 400 (or 4 x 400, 4 x 800, 4 x 400), with 90 sec between intervals, extra 90 sec between sets
H5	'Bondarenko' session. 4000m + 2000m. Each 2000m section is run as follows: 400m (5km pace), 400 steady, 300m (1500 pace), 300 steady, 200m (800m pace), 200 steady, 100m sprint, 100m jog. After the first 2000 the runner goes straight into the next one, but after that he has 5 min recovery jog before the next 2000m. The full Bondarenko session consists of 6000-4000-2000, and the running between the fast bits is kept fast enough so that each 2000m section occupies only 6 minutes.

Equally tough is the 'Brendan Foster' session , where you alternately sprint 50 metres and jog 50 metres, doing this four times per lap. One mile of this is tough, 8 laps of it is very hard indeed, but Brendan says that he once ran 5000m like this and did it in 13.30!

The structure of a two-week cycle would look like this:

Mon	Easy 7-8 miles plus strides
Tue	M1
Wed	H1
Thu	Easy 8 miles
Fri	M4
Sat	H2
Sun	10-12 miles endurance run
Mon	Easy fartlek run
Tue	M2 or M3
Wed	H 4 or H5
Thu	2 x (8 x 200)
Fri	Rest or 30 min jog
Sat	Race
Sun	Endurance run, 10-12 miles

Nnenna Lynch (USA), coached by the author, coming second in the AAA championships 5000m.

Track schedule 6

International level 5000/10,000m runner. Target times sub- 13.30/28.00 (men), sub 15.00/31.00 (women)

To reach this level the runner will already have been training hard for several years and will be able to cope with 80-100 miles (120-160km) per week.

The amount of high-quality running which can be tolerated varies from one athlete to the next. One can work to a hard-easy-hard-easy pattern, or use a 3-day microcycle as in Schedule 5, or a 4-day cycle which goes Easy-Moderate-Hard-Hard. The harder the programme, the shorter the time during which it can be sustained. The one below is based on a 4-day microcycle, and is the hardest training which might be done before tapering in the two weeks before a major 10,000m race.

Mon	am 6 miles easy, pm 8 miles easy
Tue	am 10 miles good aerobic run, pm 6 miles easy
Wed	am 5 miles easy, pm 2 x (10 x 400m) in 65, 30sec recovery and 3 min between sets

Thu	am 5 miles easy, pm 5 x 1500m on grass, 3 min rest
Fri	am 5 miles easy, pm 5 miles easy
Sat	am 8 miles good aerobic run, pm 6 miles easy plus strides
Sun	am 10 x 400m hills, 10 x 60m hills, 10 x 200m strides, pm 6 miles easy
Mon	am Repetition session, 1000m-3000m-2000m-3000m-1000m, at 10km race pace, with 2 min recovery per 1000m run
Tue	Rest day
Wed	am easy 10 miles, pm 5 miles plus strides
Thu	am 8 miles Fartlek, doing 2 min fast, 3 min steady
Fri	am 3 x (10 x 200m) in 30-32 sec with 30 sec recovery, 400 jog between sets
Sat	7 x (1000 + 400), with 1 min before the 400, 2 min 30 after it. The 1000 at 10km race pace, the 400 at 5km race pace
Sun	One run, 15 miles

The alternative to this is to follow Schedule 5, but add an extra run every day and make the hard sessions harder.

Chapter 12

Staying fit

Once you have made the effort to get fit, it makes no sense to let that fitness disappear. You can spend years building a runner's body, but within twelve months of giving up you will have lost most of what you have gained. On the other hand, a sensible maintenance programme will enable you to stay at around eighty per cent of full fitness, so that you will only be a few weeks away from peak fitness.

Complete inactivity is disastrous. A leg put into plaster can lose an inch in thigh circumference in the first twenty-four hours. Fortunately, this rarely happens. When we have been training hard and we rest up, our condition actually improves for the first two days. The chief benefit is in the stores of fuel in the muscle, in the form of glycogen. These are depleted when we do a long run – somewhere around 50% depleted by a ten-mile run, 95% depleted by a twenty-mile run. The 50% depletion will be fully made up in twenty-four hours, provided that you take in plenty of carbohydrate and water soon after your run (see Diet, Chapter 5), but the depletion of a really long run will take at least 48 hours to make good. Most serious runners will have two really easy days before a hard race and in many cases they take it easy for three or four days before a big race. The difference between 'rest' and 'taking it easy' depends on your lifestyle. If you have an active day involving quite a lot of

walking or stairclimbing, you don't need to do any running, because your walking will use the muscles enough to get the blood capillaries opening up and the fuel stores will be replenished. If you have a very sedentary lifestyle, a gentle run of twenty or thirty minutes is a good idea. In general, 'active rest' is better than 'couch-potato mode'.

If we are thinking of a short break during a hard period of training or competition, then 'active rest' for up to six days will do no harm, but there are particular times when a break has to be taken and these should be planned for.

After a marathon

In the first week you need do nothing at all except walk. In the second week you should be combining walking and gentle jogging. If you feel good you can get back to regular running in that week, but I would suggest that this need not come until the third week, when you get back to half or two-thirds of a normal mileage. By the fourth week you should be training normally, and if you have handled your recuperation properly you should be running really well six weeks after your marathons. It *is* important not to push yourself in the two weeks immediately following the race.

137

Between one season and the next

No competitive runner should be trying to compete all the year round. As I said in Chapter 4, it is best to have a training period which leads up to a definite racing programme and then to have a break when the racing season has finished. This break is essential, in my opinion, if the whole system – muscles, brain, heart and hormones – is to revitalize itself for the next big effort. In the British pattern there is only a short time in the spring between the end of the cross-country and the beginning of the track season, during which time there are road races and road relays. The 'maintenance' in this period must have enough volume in it to maintain aerobic fitness and endurance, since heavy demands are soon going to be made on the system. I would suggest that the routine be: one week of 'active rest', running no more than 30 minutes a day, three or four times a week; one week of mainly easy running with at least one session of 10 x 200m, untimed, followed by the first week of preparation for the track season, taken fairly casually (see Chapter 11).

When the break comes at the end of a tough summer season of racing, whether on road or track, a much longer rest can be taken. One of my athletes, the Kenyan Mike Boit, used to do nothing at all from September to the end of November, and he had one of the longest international track careers of anyone. The classic example is that of Cosmos N'Deti, who won the Boston Marathon for the second time in 1994 and then took several months off, in which time he gained twenty pounds. He started getting fit again in the autumn, got back into serious training after Christmas and won Boston again in 1995 to make it three in a row.

The ambitious young athlete comes off the track season in August and very often hurls himself into mileage build-up in early September. By mid-October he is very fit. This may be fine if he is going into the short American cross-country season, but in Europe, where the peak performances of the winter are needed in February and March, it is usually a mistake.

It is much better to give yourself three or four weeks of not worrying about running at all. Better to refresh the body and mind with something completely different – reading some books perhaps, a visit to the theatre, or going abroad. In this way, when you get back into the routine, even though you may find it more difficult for the first couple of weeks, the running will be more of a challenge – and you may have a few different things to think about. If you have had four weeks of hardly running at all, you must expect to need another four weeks of training before you approach full fitness. A suitable routine would be to start with only 50% of your normal training volume, at 50% effort, and then move up to 60, 70 and 80% in volume, increasing the amount of hard running a little each week.

Old runners never die – they just get shorter!

Injuries

A man's greatest strength is often his greatest weakness and this is particularly noticeable amongst full-time sportsmen and women. The compulsive streak in their character which drives them to practice hour after hour, day after day, is their worst enemy when it comes to handling injuries. The only way around this is to put 'avoidance of injury' high on the list of priorities.

When I am making out a training plan, I always start with the objectives – such things as improving aerobic fitness, practising changes of pace or maintaining flexibility. Including 'avoidance of injury' in this list brings it into the reckoning when planning a week's training. These are my guidelines.

1.	Never train hard when stiff from the previous effort
2.	Introduce new activities very gradually
3.	Allow lots of time for warming up and cooling off
4.	Check over training and competition courses beforehand
5.	Train on different surfaces, using the right footwear
6.	Shower and change immediately after the cool-down
7.	Aim for the maximum comfort when travelling
8.	Stay away from infectious areas when training or competing very hard
9.	Be extremely fussy about hygiene in hot weather
10.	Monitor the athlete daily for signs of fatigue. If in doubt, ease off.

Never train hard, when stiff

This seems obvious, but it is seen all too often at the beginning of a season or in a training camp. Some people turn up very fit and set a fast pace in training – and the others suffer for it the next day, but instead of waiting for the stiffness to go, they try to go on training as hard as the day before. The result is that running is awkward, movements are not coordinated and injuries are more likely.

Introduce new activities gradually

Ideally, one would never introduce anything new at all, but there is a first time for everything and there are bound to be changes of emphasis – such as the switch from indoor to outdoor training, or from grass to a synthetic surface. The solution is to start switching well before it is necessary. In switching from cross-country running to the synthetic track, for example, one might include a bit of running on the track whenever the opportunity arises, even if it is only three or four laps and a few strides. The first track session of the year would only be half a normal session, and it would be done mostly in trainers. The following week one might do most of one session on the track, but only part of it in spikes, and for the next two weeks one increases the proportion done in spikes. After a month we might be running three times a week on the track, with other sessions being done mostly on grass.

Warming up and cooling down

In the British climate this is particularly necessary. Warm muscles stretch much better than cold muscles. Ligaments and tendons are more likely to tear when the muscles are cold and inflexible. The warm-up procedure helps in several other ways, too, both physically, in diverting the blood flow from non-essential areas to working muscles and mentally, in focusing the sportsman on the approaching event.

I would recommend at least fifteen minutes and up to thirty minutes warm-up before hard training starts. In ball games this can often be done with a ball, carrying out various skill routines, but in all cases it should start with five to ten minutes of gentle movement, gradually increasing in pace, followed by five to ten minutes of stretching, still in warm clothing. After that one moves to fast strides and eventually to short sprints. Above all, stay warm and loose until the start. A sprinter might well take forty-five minutes to warm up for a ten-second burst of energy. During the cool-down period, which should last for ten to fifteen minutes after a competition or a hard training session, the body temperature returns to normal and the fatigue products are flushed out of the muscles, which reduces the chances of stiffness the next day.

Check the course beforehand

In cross-country and road running there may be unexpected traps for the unwary – pot-holes in the road, sudden ups or downs, all of which could cause trouble if you are not prepared for them, and of course this is closely linked to the next rule.

Wear the right shoes

Wearing shoes which are too light and flimsy or which are unevenly worn are two very common causes of injury. If you turn up expecting a soft course and find that it is frozen hard, you could be in a lot of trouble. I once arrived for a so-called cross-country race in Madrid to find that it was

90% road; luckily I had brought my road racing shoes, but my England colleague, who had only spikes, had to run the race in dance shoes strapped on with pink ribbon! At a higher level, Liz McColgan threw away a chance of winning the World Cross-Country title in Boston because she had not checked out the length of spikes necessary on the snow-covered course.

Perhaps the commonest cause of all injuries is training too much on hard surfaces. Running fast on roads and tartan tracks causes a lot of impact shock. I recommend getting off the road at least one day in three.

There is no such thing as bad weather – merely unsuitable clothing.

Shower and change after training

This reduces the likelihood of stiffening up and your chances of catching a cold. Ideally, a hard session or a race should always be followed by a massage, if you want to recover quickly.

Travel in comfort

This sounds a bit cissy, but it is not at all uncommon for athletes to stay wedged into a minibus or a train, sitting awkwardly for several hours before an important event. I recommend that you get up, walk around and stretch once every hour while travelling, if possible. Apart from the muscles, the more you can keep down the stress, the better you will perform. It is best to get to the venue the day before the event for anything big, and if you have to deal with big changes in climate and/or time zones, it is best to be there a week beforehand.

Avoid infection

After hard sessions the immune system is definitely vulnerable. Sportsmen in hard training are particularly susceptible before a big event. They should stay away from crowded rooms, schools and people with bad colds.

Be fussy about hygiene

All too often people in training camps or in Games villages pick up 'stomach bugs' just before the big event, and the reason is often evident from the sloppy conditions in which they live, with food left around, dirty clothing, people sharing cups and glasses. Athletes, like most young people, have a sense of invulnerability which is positively dangerous.

Monitor fatigue

This has been dealt with in earlier issues, but it cannot be too highly stressed. In hindsight it is usually possible to trace the cause of an illness or an injury, and there is usually a point where the athlete *should* have eased off but didn't. It is a vital part of the coach's job to tell the athlete when to stop, and the athlete must play his part by being aware of the early signs of over-tiredness; a raised resting pulse is one sure sign.

Attitude to injury

However careful you are, injuries can occur, particularly in the stress of competition, and illnesses can be picked up, often when the athlete is really fit.

The first thing is damage limitation. The usual course of events is as follows:

1. The athlete feels a little pain during training and ignores it.
2. The pain recurs, and may even be felt after training, but is not bad enough to prevent training.
3. The pain is now bad enough to interfere with normal training, but the athlete can still compete, if he rests.
4. The pain is so bad that the athlete can neither train nor compete.

The time to report the injury and to start treatment is at Stage One. The procedure should be to switch right away from any exercise which makes the injury more painful and to get diagnosis immediately, certainly not later than the next day. At the same time, coach and athlete should work out what forms of exercise are possible and redesign the programme so that the athlete is at least doing something to maintain cardiovascular fitness, maintain constant body weight and muscle strength. An inactive injured athlete is a real 'sick gorilla'. It is as important to maintain his morale and confidence as it is to maintain his fitness, but in these days of leisure centres, gyms, static bikes and aquajoggers it is always possible to find some suitable exercise.

To take an example, I had a case where a runner was tripped and fell, tearing some fibres just below the kneecap, three weeks before the Olympic Trials. After icing it and protecting it for the first two days, he started on daily physiotherapy, and massaged the area before each session, to stimulate the blood flow. He couldn't cycle with it, but he could walk, do some circuit training and swim front crawl. After three days of this he progressed to walking and jogging on grass, then to long uphill jogs, trying to avoid limping. Running uphill on grass means that there is very little stress, but the heart is working quite hard. By the tenth day he was doing long slow training, by the fourteenth day he was able to train hard, but still mainly uphill on grass.

In the third week he was able to do part of the session on the track and at the end of the week he went into the trials with no knee problem at all and finished second, qualifying for the Olympic team.

The key is rapid action and a lot of psychological support to back up the remedial treatment. It is when things are not going well that the athlete really needs his coach.

Training Alternatives

1. **Treadmill running.** Sometimes you can run on a treadmill without aggravating your injury, and as this is the closest thing to real running, it is excellent training, particularly since it can be accurately controlled. Start with short bouts of walking and jogging, then progress to faster speeds and steeper gradients as you feel you can cope.

2. **Cycling.** The exercise bike is the runner's best friend when he has a back injury, and sometimes it can be used for ankle and shin injuries too. It is said that cycling most closely resembles the running action when you are standing up rather than sitting down. Like the treadmill, it can be carefully calibrated and you can do either endurance sessions or a form of interval training, when you are working hard, with a high work load, for periods of one to three minutes, followed by easy periods.

3. **Training in the pool.** Since the invention of the 'wet vest' and other support-ing devices, in-the-pool training has become more useful to runners. For years, swimming has been recommended for injured runners as a way of maintaining cardiovascular fitness without putting weight onto injured joints, but with a flotation vest the runner can remain in an upright position and run on the spot against the resistance of the water. This can be done in bursts, like the cycling, so the runner can get a proper training workout.

4. **Weight training.** With a well-equipped gym, the runner can do useful training by working on all the muscles except the ones which are injured. To avoid over-development of the body, weights should only be done two or three times a week and combined with cardiovascular exercise.

5. **Circuit training.** From the exercise given in Appendix D, the runner can select those which are possible; this will give another alternative and add variety to the training.

RUNNING IS EASY

The nicer the surroundings, the easier it is to run.

Staying fit while under pressure

There are times in our lives when running must take a back seat, because of pressure of work, moving house, travelling long distances or simply the demands of the family. To insist on maintaining a full training and racing programme may be selfish and insensitive or downright impossible, but it should be possible to retain a degree of fitness. With three or four half-hour sessions a week you can

hang onto most of the fitness you have built up when training properly. If you have been in the habit of racing a lot, the break may even do you good and prevent chronic injuries from building up.

There are various strategies. Firstly, when under pressure, use a run for therapy. It doesn't matter what time of the day or night you go out, as long as you can get thirty minutes on your own. Start running easily, don't worry about the pace, and just try to clear your mind. As you go along, think of the best running moments you have had, and remember that you still have the rest of your life to enjoy running. If you find yourself picking up the pace, fine, if you just want to jog, fine; taking your body out for a run will remind it of what it is used to.

Secondly, find the time to run or walk by using your feet in the city, rather than the car or the public transport. Ten minutes of jogging and brisk walking, two or three times a day, and your maintenance training is done.

Thirdly, once a week, try to get to an open space where you can put in twenty minutes of speed work. This is more effective than anything else in keeping up your fitness. A mile of jogging, a couple of minutes of stretching and you can go straight into twenty times 'thirty seconds fast, thirty seconds slow'. This is a really good workout, believe me.

Fourthly, if you are stuck in the house, say looking after a sick child, you can do an indoor circuit which will maintain muscle tone and do something for cardiovascular fitness. Make each activity no more than a minute long, but work hard in that minute and move onto the next one as soon as possible.

Six Indoor Circuit exercises

1. Skipping (or bouncing if you have no rope)
2. Pushups
3. Running on the spot with high knee lift
4. Hanging onto the stairs and doing pull-ups
5. Squat-thrusts or Burpees
6. Sit-ups

Age and the runner

When we are young we feel immortal, and in a sense we are, because our cells renew themselves constantly. For some reason cells eventually lose their power to regenerate. As the rate of cell division slows down some tissues begin to perform less efficiently. There is a loss of elasticity, both in the skin and in the ligaments. There is a decline in the maximum heart rate and in the maximum power output of muscles. If the athlete trains conscientiously, it is possible to retain both flexibility and strength for much longer than was previously supposed. In recent years we have seen that sprinters such as Linford Christie, Carl Lewis, Calvin Smith and Merlene Ottey can go on performing at the very highest level into their mid-thirties. In the longer events it has been shown that you can stay in world class until the age of forty. Carlos Lopes won the World Cross-Country title and the Olympic Marathon at the age of 37; Eamonn Coghlan ran under four minutes for the mile at 40 and in 1994 the Russian athlete Podkopaeva won several Grand Prix races and finished third in the European 1500 metres championships at the age of 42.

Longevity of performance is most impressive in the marathon, because endurance is so susceptible to the effects of training. Joyce Smith and Priscilla Welch both set British records, below 2 hr 30 when in their forties, Jack Foster of New Zealand won the silver medal in the Commonwealth Games Marathon, with a

It's good to be an athlete when you are thirty, but it is essential when you are over fifty.

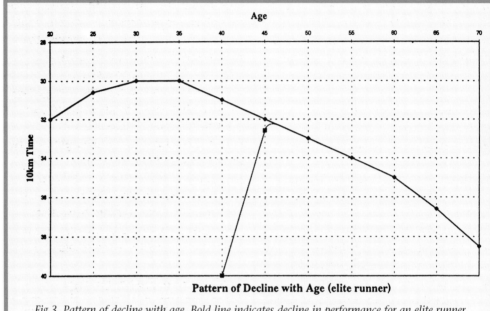

Pattern of Decline with Age (elite runner)

Fig 3. Pattern of decline with age. Bold line indicates decline in performance for an elite runner, while shadow line shows pattern for runner starting at age 40.

time of under 2 hr 12 and his over-40 record was recently improved by John Campbell, also of New Zealand, to just over 2 hr 11 min.

We could take examples from cycling, from weightlifting and from dancing to show that by consistent training people in their forties, fifties and even sixties can perform at a level far above that of the average twenty-five-year-old, but eventually decline is bound to set in. As more and more people take part in veteran or 'Masters' sports, data is accumulating about the rate of this decline. It is of the order of 0.5% per year in strength and speed.

A look at my own training diary will give you an idea. I ran the equivalent of 13.45 for 5000 metres in 1960 and continued at around that level, sometimes a little faster, until I retired in 1967. After this my training level dropped. Instead of training hard almost every day I continued to run regularly and just trained hard when I felt like it – sometimes once a week, sometimes less often. In 1971, aged 35, I ran 14.28 for 5000m and twenty years later I ran 16.19 – a decline of 109 seconds. In the Hyde Park fun run, four kilometres on grass, I slowed from 12.20 to 13.40 over 15 years. Over 10km on the road I have declined from being a 29.00 man in 1967 (aged 32) to running 32.30 in 1985 (aged

50) and 35.00 in 1994; this is a decline of 360 seconds over 27 years and 150 seconds in the last nine years. Comparing the three distances we get the following rates of decline:

4km on grass   1.3 sec/km/year
5km on track   1.1 sec/km/year
10km on road   1.3 sec/km/year

Rounding things up, we can reckon on a steady rate of decline, after the age of 35, of about 1.3 sec/km/year or 2 sec/mile/year, which is 0.55% per year. This means that over 5 years, other things being equal, you will slow down by 1 minute over 10km and 2 minutes in a half-marathon.

The exception to this is the 'born-again' runner. When someone comes new to the sport, or takes it up again after twenty years or more, there is a huge surge of

Interval training is the quickest way of getting fit.

enthusiasm and although the runner is getting older, his performances will continue to improve for several years, because the improvements due to training are greater than the decline due to ageing.

There is no doubt that the average person (which means, by our standards, an unfit person) can reverse many of the effects of ageing by using the right exercise programme and remain younger, in the physiological sense, than his real age. At the time of writing, just short of my sixtieth birthday, I am running the sort of times that I was doing in my first year of competition, as a 19-year-old soldier.

Doing the right thing

What are the implications of the for the average sportsman?

Firstly, there is no reason to stop doing what you enjoy purely because of your age. As long as you can do it, you are not too old to do it.

Secondly, it is neither necessary nor desirable to train with the same intensity as the younger athlete. After years of training, your body is not going to undergo any radical change unless you stop training completely. It is more a matter of keeping your weight down and your body ticking over and then putting in a few weeks of more serious training before a big event. Since the rate of regeneration is not as fast, the older athlete will need more time between hard sessions. Speaking personally, I find it hard to motivate myself more than two or three times a year, but I can train hard, 2 or 3 times a week, on those rare occasions.

Thirdly, it will probably become necessary to work on your weak points if you want to remain fit and healthy. Since muscular strength and flexibility both decline, it is a good thing to do sessions which emphasize these. It is necessary for the specialist sportsman to become less of a specialist, in order to retain the all-round fitness he took for granted when young. The runner should spend more time on upper body training and the swimmer should spend more time on his feet.

None of us is immortal. We are programmed to die – otherwise evolution would not occur – but we should train to live. An old New Orleans jazz man, when he reached his 100th birthday, said: 'If I'd known I was going to live this long, I'd have taken better care of myself!'

It is a good thing to be an athlete at forty, but it is essential at seventy. My own goal is the centenarian marathon record. It is far enough away to make hard training unnecessary, but as a distant goal it gives me the incentive not to lose what I have got from the last forty years of regular running. It doesn't matter if I never achieve it, so long as I gain from the effort I make. We always need a goal to make life significant – and the joy of being a runner is that you always have one. If you have done nothing else today, you can still feel satisfied if you have been for your run.

The problem which the ageing athlete faces is that the culture of sport is based on the 'young warrior' concept. The youth prepares for his initiation into adult games. The young adult strives to prove himself, to move up into the ranks of the battle-hardened warriors. In sporting terms he tries to move from local success into the national arena and if he succeeds there he moves onto the international scene, culminating in a World Championships or Olympic Games.

Whatever level he reaches, there comes a time when improvement stops. By the use of experience he may be able to stay at the same level of performance through his mid-thirties, even up to the age of forty in a few cases, but decline eventually sets in. In the

No matter what your approach, you should be able to find the right level of competition, whether you're male or female.

animal world the old bull is driven out by the young bulls. In the tribal world the warrior becomes an elder and is no longer expected to fight. In the sporting world the former champion is supposed to retire with his laurels. This is where the problem lies. How does the athlete who has always motivated himself with the idea of continual improvement cope with the inevitability of steady decline?

The 'Bannister' approach

Roger Bannister, the first man to break four minutes for the Mile, achieved this feat in May 1954, when he was 25 years old and had just qualified as a doctor. Later that summer he went on to become European champion at 1500 metres and Commonwealth champion at the Mile, defeating John Landy, the man who had reduced the world mile record to 3 min 57.9 sec. Bannister retired from athletics at the end of that summer, acknowledged as the supreme middle-distance runner of his era, and went on to a distinguished career in medicine. Although he has continued to promote the ideals of physical fitness, he never competed again, preferring to put all his energies into his career and his family life.

The 'Mike McLeod' approach

Mike McLeod is best known for winning a silver medal in the Olympic 10,000 metres in 1984, but his consistency and durability are perhaps even more remarkable. Now 43, his international career has lasted for twenty years and he is still a major force in road races in the North-East. There are races which he has won for more than ten years in a row, but he still turns out, defying the years, and as competitive as ever.

The 'Steve James' approach

Steve James was a brilliant junior athlete and was labelled as 'the new Bannister' in his first year at Oxford. However, he put his academic and professional goals first and re-emerged on the running scene in his late forties. Since then he has gone on to win numerous World titles in veteran competition, setting British veteran records at 5000 and 10,000 metres.

These are just three examples – and naturally I have chosen those who are prominent and successful. Each of these men has

Races are the best incentive for staying fit.

achieved great things in the sport, showing what can be done. Each has gained satisfaction from the sport in his own way, and who is to say that one way is better than the other?

As long as you choose to compete, the competition is there. Every five years you enter a new age band in veteran competition. There are clubs which run veteran teams, there are British, European and World championships on the track and on the road, at all distances, and there are even international cross-country matches for veterans.

Most of us, however, do not aim this high. We like to run, we like to feel fit and in command of our bodies. Running in the occasional race adds spice to the training and winning an age-group prize is good for the self-esteem.

The secret is not to dwell on what you did ten or twenty years ago, but to look forward to what you are going to do this year. There are always new places to go, races you have never run, and a veteran can enjoy these things in a way that the younger runner, burdened with expectation and ambition, never can. The older runner can enjoy a glass of wine with his meal the night before; he can afford the time to make friends with his fellow athletes. If he wants to take a day off training and go for a walk in the hills, he can. The physical fitness you have built up over the years is like a treasure you have built up – but it must not be hoarded in a miserly way. Paradoxically, the more you expend, the more you have left.

Nuts and bolts

On a practical note, there is no reason why an older runner should not follow any of the schedules I have given, but he must be prepared to take more time over them. He will need more easy days in between the hard days. He must be careful to warm up and to warm down properly – in other words, to treat himself like a serious athlete. This attitude may seem a little selfish – but your children and your grand-children, if they think about it, would rather you were active and independent, if slightly quirky, than a candidate for the Zimmer frame.

What I hope that we have learned by this stage in life is that running is primarily a means of survival. Staying fit and healthy should always be more important than any single race. Running is just one way of keeping a physical and mental balance and to take it too seriously at this stage in life is a little unbalanced – so beware of becoming a running bore. The philosophy which I would recommend is that expressed by Tennyson in his poem *Ulysses*; some of the lines are particularly appropriate to older runners:

'Though much is taken, much abides,
    and though
We are not now that strength which in old days
Moved earth and heaven, that which we are,
    we are;
One equal temper of heroic hearts,
Made weak by time and fate, but strong in will,
To strive, to seek, to find and not to yield.'

Chapter 13

Running to win

The principles of successful distance racing apply to all events, whether on the track, on the road or over the country. There are differences in one's tactics depending on the length of the race and the nature of the surface, which will be dealt with in the appropriate sections, but the preparation for the race, in both physical and psychological terms, is basically the same.

Keep it simple

Ninety per cent of a victory is decided before the runners line up for the race. All the tapering, carbo-loading and psychological preparation in the world will not enable a man who cannot break 33 minutes for 10km to finish ahead of one who regularly runs it in under 30 minutes. The combination of natural ability and training will put you into a certain performance bracket. You will always finish ahead of people in the lower brackets and you will always finish behind those in the upper brackets – unless by consistent training you can move up there with them. The best way to win is to be the best runner in the race.

The talented athlete, developing at school or club level, will eventually reach a point where he is the best in his group. He knows it and the others know it, so when he stands on the start line he is, barring accidents, certain to win. He will then move on to County, State or Regional level. If he has a lot of ability, he may establish himself as the best runner there, but eventually he will reach a situation – probably a national championship – where he is only one amongst many good runners. Sooner or later, everyone reaches a point where winning is not a certainty and it is then that the race becomes really interesting.

The structure of the year

Few things are more important than this. If you just bash on with your training and

An athlete who knows all about running to win – Britain's Linford Christie.

151

take on every race that comes along, season by season, you will improve for a while, but eventually you will find yourself in a rut, doing the same training week after week. Some time in the year you should sit down with your coach, or with another runner if you have no coach, and decide what you are going to go for in the next twelve months. Every three months you should review your plan and revise it if necessary. It is possible to have three racing seasons a year, with a peak period in each one, but two peak periods a year are more common. You must allow time after each racing period for rest and recuperation, otherwise there is a danger of over-use injuries building up. When you start a new phase there will be a build-up period, four to six weeks, followed by a distinct pre-competition training period which will last from six to eight weeks – longer if altitude training is included – and then the competition period, which might extend for another six weeks. If there is a long track season one might have four weeks of early competition, then a short training period and then another few weeks of competition.

The advantage of this approach is that you are at times building up mental and physical strength without dissipating it by continuous racing. Because your racing period is short and well-defined, you go into each race with a sense of excitement and purpose.

An example of this from recent experience was Richard Nerurkar's 1993 programme, which went as follows:

Jan-Feb-March: Cross-country. Won the National Championships but had to withdraw from the World Championships team because of a virus.

April: Altitude training, part of marathon build-up.

May: Won debut marathon (2 hr 10.57) and after one easy week went into track preparation.

June-July: Track season, getting times of 27 min 40.0 (10,000m) and 13 min 30.0 (5000m), as precursor of marathon training.

August-September-October: Marathon preparation, including three weeks at altitude, culminating in a Ten -Mile record (46.02) on October 17th and victory in the World Cup Marathon (2.10.03) on October 31st.

November: Easy month.

December: Started mileage build-up before going to Kenya for altitude training on 21 Dec.

It seems as if we have crammed a lot into this year, but there was always a purpose. The cross-country season included marathon training, so that one could follow the other. Because of the virus, Richard had to postpone his marathon by two weeks, which allowed less rest before the track season. The track season in itself was only part of the plan to peak for the marathon in October, so although he set a personal best for 10,000m, he was outside his best times at the shorter distances.

The year was not an unbroken run of success for Richard. The virus affected him

Grand Prix athletics is professional running at its most competitive.

badly in the early part of the year, so we had to be flexible about choosing races. He was hoping to peak for the 5000m at the Zurich Weltklasse meeting, but we mistimed our descent from altitude and he finished a disastrous 17th. However, we knew that the overall training was going well and so were able to produce a peak performance in the most important race of the year, in October. As long as you keep your major goals in mind, making decisions is not hard.

Physical preparation

If you have read Chapter 3 you will know that the training process consists of putting the body under stress, then allowing time for the body to respond. By gradually increasing the stress and allowing time for the response we can make the body both stronger and more efficient. In the period before a race you have to know when to stop the hard training and rest, in order to get the maximum benefit from it.

Your endurance is built up over a long period and it also declines slowly. In the marathon schedules you will find that the last really long run comes three weeks before the big day. The major factors affecting your running speed, such as your flexibility, the strength of your heart, the development of blood capillaries in your leg muscles, will also change very gradually, over a period of weeks. Thus, the training you do today will not improve your performance tomorrow. My rule of thumb is that it takes at least two weeks for the benefits of a training session to show up as improvement. If you have been going through a hard training period, putting in hard efforts three or four times a week for a month, it may well be another month before you see a real improvement in race performance. If you could produce a score for 'physical condition', then it would be well below average on the day after a hard training week, but given sufficient rest, the score would rise every day, reaching a peak somewhere between the fourth and the seventh day. It would then level off for a day or two and then start to fall.

For this reason our training is divided into different phases and there must be time allowed between the hardest training period and the important races. As we approach the big race day, the volume of the training decreases and there are longer intervals between the hard days. Instead of making a training effort of an hour every day, the efforts are confined to twenty or thirty minutes and sufficient rest is given for the runner to be fresh when making the efforts. We finally come to a 'racing only' period, where the runner is racing, say, twice a week, with the other days being used for recovery only. If there are not enough races available, the runner does timed runs which simulate the racing experience. He thus becomes used to expending all his energy in the relatively short intense effort of a race.

This preparation is partly mental, but it becomes effective through the orchestration of the hormones, the enzymes and the muscle fuels, all of which must perform in harmony with the uptake and transport of oxygen. The production of the right hormones at the right time is linked to the mental preparation, but the production of the maximum number of enzymes, essential for rapid release of energy, can be encouraged by a 'zapping' session. In this the runner must be running at slightly faster than VO2 Max. pace, i.e., at 1500m racing speed. It is not necessary to run very far, but a session of 15-20 x 200m, done three days before the race, produces the right effect.

Training is specific to the event, and so as the event approaches, more and more of the training must be in the same rhythm as the race. Apart from the 'zapping' session mentioned above, I do not think that there is any value in the traditional method of making the last session before a major race one of very fast runs over a fraction of the distance. Three days before a 5000 metres race, for example, it would be better to run 3 x 800m at your projected race pace rather than 6 x 400m at five seconds a lap faster than race pace.

Tactical rehearsal

This satisfies both the mental and the physical needs of preparation. In the last few weeks before a big race one puts in sessions which simulate not only the pace but also the likely scenarios which will develop. The cross-country runner can practice putting in a burst off the top of a hill, the road runner can rehearse the mid-race surges he may encounter and the track runner can practice 'winding up' the last kilometre or accelerating in the last 200 metres. If you can simulate the kind of going you will meet, the gradient and the twists and turns of a course, you will be better able to respond in the right way during the actual race. If you can get a training partner to act out the different roles – the front runner or the 'long kicker', for example – you will be even better prepared. Read the section on race tactics and you will see what is needed.

Psychological preparation

A common question is: 'How do the great runners manage to produce their best performances on the big occasions?' The sub-text to this is that the ordinary runner never quite knows when he is going to produce his best performance. Of course, it is one of the marks of the great athlete that he rises to the occasion. This may be because his ability is so great that it is only fully utilized when the pressure is on, but more often the difference between the good athlete and the champion athlete is only a psychological one and we all know of cases where a runner can produce superb training performances but not deliver the goods in the big event.

The building of physical strength and mental strength go hand in hand. In one of my favourite Ernest Bramah stories, the hero is a coward who goes to the wise man to ask for something to give him courage. The wise man prescribes three potions. The first one requires perseverance and a little courage in collecting the various ingredients; the next one involves a more hazardous journey and a bit more courage.

When he has taken the second potion he is really determined to get the materials for the last one. The crucial ingredient is a powder made of ground-up molar teeth from a mother tiger and our hero is so keen to get it that he walks straight into the tiger's lair, stands no nonsense from the tiger and whips out the teeth he requires. Needless to say, he finds, on drinking the potion, that he has acquired the gift of courage.

Applying this to the athlete, the secret is to start with training which is challenging but achievable. When this has been mastered, the coach increases the load and goes on doing so step by step. When the training is hard enough, the races seem easy. Most of the best runners can recall a training session they have done which, on looking back, seemed awesome, but which gave them the necessary confidence in their ability.

The crucial factor in mental preparation is building confidence. If the runner believes that he is getting better he will not be afraid to reach out for the next step. It is for this reason that I recommend doing a lot of the training off the track. If the runner is doing reps over a circuit which takes four-and-a-half minutes to run and he reduces his average to 4 min 20, he

All these runners are in with a chance, but how many have a real race plan?

knows he is improving. If he was doing these on the track, he might discover that his mile reps have improved from 4.48 to 4.38, and then discover that somebody else was running them in 4.25, which would be depressing. We are always hearing about the amazing training sessions that people are supposed to have done, though, strangely enough, you never actually see them being done. If you concentrate on improving by your own standards you can ignore what other people are doing.

Focusing

This simple technique will help you produce your best form on the day when you want it. When you make out your training plan before the season starts, you will underline the one or two major events. When you are psyching yourself up to doing one more mile repetition, think of that day in the future. When you are undecided whether to ignore an injury or have it treated, think of being right for the big day. As the day approaches, try to free yourself of other commitments. That day is the horizon of your endeavour. If you know deep down that you are going to make a superhuman effort, on that day you will find it much easier to draw on your strength when it is needed.

Race-day preparation

For the true competitor, going into a race is an exalting experience. What does it feel like? If you have to ask, you'll never know.

It is something of the feeling you get when hearing Pavarotti in full voice, except that it is like *being* Pavarotti. When you are in the leading bunch, waiting to make your move, it is like being in the trenches, waiting to go over the top. When you are out in front with a mile to go and the crowd are roaring it is like being a stag on the moor, running for your life, both terrifying and exhilarating. When you cross the line in first place all life's problems disappear.

In the few hours before the race, runner and coach have to tread a fine line between being methodical and being over-fussy. Business-like is the right phrase, but the routine of the preparation should not be so rigid as to snuff out that joy of competition. Firstly, travel arrangements should be made well in advance, aiming to get you to the venue with plenty of time to spare. If the journey is long you should make sure that you get food and drink at the right time (see Chapter 14). For cross-country and road races it is best to look over the whole course beforehand and if there is not time for that, study the map closely so that you know what to expect and warm up over the last mile, so that you know exactly where the finish is.

Warming up. Your warm-up routine will usually start thirty minutes before the event and follow a routine which you have practised in training. In cool climates I recommend:

10-15 min easy jogging
5 min general stretching

1995 London Marathon winners Dionicio Ceron (MEX) and Margareta Sobanska (POL).

Put on racing shoes and do 8 x 50m strides, starting easily and working up to a fast stride by the sixth, then easing down on the last two.

Report in to the starting area and keep warm until called up. If the start is delayed, carry on jogging and stretching and remain calm. Don't waste energy on cursing the officials or the other competitors, just focus on maintaining your state of readiness, staying warm but not getting hot, taking liquid if you need it, doing enough jogging and loosening to be ready when called.

Racing strategy. In many domestic races, the winner is simply the man or woman who is the best prepared, but when you reach national and international level you need more than just ability and fitness. Just performing well will not guarantee you a win, because there are several others who have the ability to win.

To win the race you need:

1. The intention of winning.
2. A plan (or several plans)of how to win
3. The determination and ability to carry out your plan.
4. A little luck – or the absence of bad luck.

Let us take a specific race, the Commonwealth Games 1500m final of 1994. There was no clear favourite – none of the leading Kenyans was entered and Simon Doyle of Australia, who might have been the favourite, was injured.

In the field we had David Strang of Scotland, the World Indoor champion, Kevin McKay, the English champion, John Mayock of England, the World Student Games champion Hood, and Sullivan of Canada, who carried the expectations of the home crowd along with three young Africans, Achon of Uganda and Chesang and Tanui of Kenya, who were expected to

157

uphold their countries' distance running tradition.

You will never win a race unless you put yourself in a position from which you can win.

If you have the finishing speed of Billy Konchellah you might be able to get away with trailing along at the back of the field until the last lap, but very few can do this.

The usual Kenyan race tactics are to nominate the most junior member of the team to set the pace. On this occasion Tanui and Achon set a pace which was fast enough to discourage McKay and Strang, both renowned 'kickers' in slow races. Going down the back straight in the last lap, neither of these two was within striking distance. If the leaders in a race of this kind run the last 200 metres in 26 seconds, someone at the back of the field would have to run it in under 25 seconds to win, as well as threading his way through the runners ahead of him. Chesang, the Kenyan first string, clearly ran to a winning plan, sticking close to his pacemakers, taking the lead from them and kicking from the front. Mayock and Sullivan, by sticking close to Chesang, put themselves into a position from which they could have won had they possessed a little more strength or finishing speed. Sullivan came round Mayock and got very close to the Kenyan, with Mayock finishing in the bronze medal position, a couple of strides behind. McKay finished 8th and Strang 12th.

It is easy to theorise about these things, but how do you achieve them when under the pressure of the race? There are several

Richard Nerurkar wins the World Cup marathon 1993, Britain's first major marathon title for 19 years.

effective techniques which can be used to help you. The first is by teamwork – as demonstrated so effectively by the Kenyans. The team is stronger than the sum of its parts. When running as an individual one often tends to hold back from maximum pace, for fear of 'blowing up', but it is possible for a runner to run harder and to hold less back when he is running for the team, because he is acting under orders and he will not be blamed if he blows up. The first string runner can run confidently behind the pacemaker, because he has always beaten him in training, so he saves his big mental effort for the last lap. Moreover, he *has* to play his part when the big moment comes, because he has had his orders. By giving the athletes instructions the coach relieves them from self-doubt, which is so often a betrayer of hope on the big occasion.

The other effective bit of teamwork is between the athlete and the coach, even though the coach is not on the track. The athlete who does it all by himself is now the exception rather than the rule. The coach does not merely study the opposition and make the plans, he builds into the athlete the conviction that he is good enough to win, that he ought to win, that he must not tolerate defeat. If the coach has experience at international level his arguments are much more convincing. Thinking back to that Commonwealth Games, it is significant that two of the British distance runners who distinguished themselves most were Mayock, coached by Peter Elliott, and Mark Hudspith, coached by the former marathon gold medallist, Jim Alder. The most successful, however, was Rob Denmark, winner of the 5000 metres, who is coached by his father. In this case, the key to Rob's self-belief was his silver medal in the European Championships a few weeks earlier.

Even if you have no coach and you are not the fastest man in the field it is possible to convince yourself that you can win. David Hemery, winner of the 1968 Olympic 400 metres hurdles race, often talks about the visual imagery he used to get himself into a winning frame of mind.

Instead of worrying about the other competitors, he concentrated on his most pleasurable runs and visualised himself running the perfect race.

The complete athlete has thought through every scenario and worked out his response. He has rehearsed in training the way in which he would react to an early breakaway or a mid-race kick. The more often he has visualised his response, the more automatic it will be. The more you see yourself winning, the more likely you are to win.

Once upon a time, a lifetime ago, I was a young lad from a Devon village, running in bare feet in the European Championships. Distance running then was dominated by the professionals from the Eastern bloc, first Zatopek and Kuts and then Bolotnikov, the Olympic 10,000m champion. The only British gold medallist had been Wooderson in 1946. I had run the times, though, and I was convinced that I could win. I had a little mantra which went: 'Who is going to win? Bruce is going to win!'

It may sound childish, but it worked.

Firstly, you must train so that you have the ability to win. Secondly, you must be convinced that you can win and thirdly, you must put yourself into a position from which you have a chance of winning.

Race tactics

800 and 1500 metres
As with any race, you must know your

own strengths and those of your opponents. There are only three basic tactics – the fast race from the front, the mid-race break and the late kick.

If you are the fastest man in the field, all you have to do is to stay close enough to the leader, run economically in the middle stages, avoid getting boxed in on the last lap and put yourself into a position to strike over the last 200 metres. This was the way in which Seb Coe won his two Olympic 1500m titles and the way in which Fermin Cacho won the Barcelona Olympics.

If you are not the fastest finisher, you should try to cooperate with someone else in the field, to share the pacemaking, and to set such a fast pace that the kickers will

Track races become more tactical, as there are more top-class performers.

not be close enough to you. Peter Elliott did this very effectively against William Tanui in Auckland in 1990, but it was best shown by Paul Ruto in the 1993 World Championships 800m, where, nominated as pacemaker for the holder, Billy Konchellah and the Olympic champion, William Tanui, he just burned off at the front, running the first 200 metres in under 25 seconds, and stayed there all the way.

The tactical burst in mid-race can only be applied if the first part of the race is slow. The person who does it has the advantage of surprise, which is worth a couple of metres, but he must also have the strength and the confidence to keep going all the way.

Running in qualifying rounds. Be sure that you know exactly what the qualifying conditions are. If you are in the last heat and you know that, say, five out of eight can qualify just by running a brisk pace, don't keep it to yourself. Get together with a couple of others and plan between you to keep up the necessary pace.

If you have the ability, it is better to go out and dominate your heat or semi-final rather than run the sensible economical race to qualify you in third place. The battle for mental domination of the final is often won on the strength of how people look in the earlier rounds. The only exception to this is in the longer races, where racing out the last 800 metres of a 5000 metres heat in hot weather may be very tiring.

Pace judgement. If you are running in a race where you have no realistic chance of winning, the best you can hope for is a fast time. When running at your limit, you should run close to level pace. In an 800 metres your first 200 should be only slightly faster than the second, and the second 400 metres should be no more than one second slower than the first. In a 1500m it is important not to make the first lap too fast, otherwise you will be running the rest of the way in oxygen debt. Physiologically, the most efficient way to run is to make the first lap exactly level pace, but usually you will have to run slightly faster to stay in touch with the race. The best way to run, say, a 3.45 1500 metres, would be to run the first three laps in 59, 60 and 61 and to accelerate to 45 sec for your last 300 metres.

5000 and 10,000 metres

These races are tougher mentally because they require concentration over a longer period. The top-class runner is running so fast all the way through that he is hurting, but he has learned to ignore the discomfort. Gordon Pirie, world record holder and Olympic silver medallist, once said to me 'in my best races I feel bad at the half-distance and I feel like dropping out at three-quarters of the distance, and then I push myself harder.'

Emil Zatopek, the only man to win the 5000m, 10,000m and marathon in the same Olympics, and one of the greatest front-runners, said 'When I feel bad, I think that the others must be feeling worse, or they would not be behind me. When I feel really terrible, I fight my hardest.'

The same principles apply as for the middle-distance events. A fast finisher like Dieter Baumann or Kahlid Skah knows that he has a good chance of winning if he is still there – at the bell – but he has to be fit enough to stay with the pace. To beat someone like Baumann the most effective tactic is to put in such fast run in the early part of the race that he dare not go with you. This was done by Yobes Ondieki in winning the Tokyo World Championships 5000. He ran very close to four minutes for four laps in the first half of the race. It is not surprising that he was out on his own by that point, but it was more surprising that he was able to stay out in front and win. Ismael Kirui won in similar fashion when running against Skah in the 1993 World Championships. However, if the 'kicker' has the strength and the self-control to cope with the breaks and stay in touch, he has a big psychological advantage in the last lap. Haile Gebresilasie of Ethiopia outkicked Moses Tanui and Richard Chelimo in the World Championships 10,000, 1993, as did Kahlid Skah in the 1992 Olympics. For every ploy there is a counter-ploy – that is what makes the battles so perennially fascinating. The great Lasse Viren, winner of four Olympic titles in 1972 and 1976, used the 'long kick' to perfection, hitting the front with about one kilometre to go and winding up the pace so much that no one could get past him.

Cross-country

Because there are so many breaks in continuity, due to hills, jumps, tight bends or changes in going, cross-country presents far more opportunities for the front runner. The tactics are really quite simple. In a big race, with a big field, you cannot afford to hang back at the start if you are hoping to win. If there are fifty people between you and the leader you will use so much energy in trying to get past them that you might as well have gone with the leaders.

On the other hand, if you are not aiming for the top six in a race you can gain a lot by running level pace. In championships races in particular, people go off much too fast and as long as the course gives enough room to pass the man who can maintain his pace in the second half of the race will be passing people all the time.

Whatever your ambitions, it is essential to look closely at the course beforehand. In Richard Nerurkar's first season of senior cross-country in Britain, his first big race was the Margate international, a Euro-Cross event. The course was flat, round playing fields, and the only variation was where it went in and out of some trees in a sharp S-bend. At this point the course also became narrower. While looking round the course we practised running into the S-bend and taking the 180-degree turn by swinging around the trees. In the second lap of the race, Richard accelerated into the

lead just before the S-bend and then ran fast through it, while the rest of the field funnelled into single file behind him. When he came out of the trees he had a thirty metre lead and, having broken contact, he then worked as hard as he could to stretch the lead before the beginning of the third and final lap. His win there gave him the confidence to approach his next race in a similarly positive way. When it came to the National cross-country in Leeds he chose the point which most people were dreading, Hill Sixty (so called because of its slope), to make his decisive break.

Races will not always go as perfectly as you plan them, but the successful cross-country runner is one who never gives up, who tries to get the most advantage out of the course at every stage. He finds out the bits he likes best and attacks on those. Above all, the cross-country man has to cultivate a feeling of irrepressibility, the knowledge, which comes from a high degree of fitness, that however tough things are, he can always bounce back.

Road racing

The road offers much more opportunity to the even-paced runner. There are fewer breaks in continuity, there is plenty of road to run in and there are plenty of people on the road. To get the best out of yourself, an even-paced run is the most efficient, so if you can to run a 33-minute 10 kilometre race you should try to go off at 3 min 20 per kilometre and no faster. It is worth experimenting in a minor race with going for a 'negative split' – that is running the second half of the race faster than the first. The advantage of this is that you feel good in the first half, and when you speed up later on you are always passing people. The disadvantage is that you may be too far back and there are big gaps to close up, where you lose your momentum.

If you are hoping to win the race you may have to sacrifice some of your level-pace ideas to stay in contact with the leaders. Since there are so many runners in the field, it is usually possible to use these as 'stepping-stones' to bring you up to the leaders when they slow down.

In a packed field the last mile of the race may become as tactical as a track race and it is vital to know exactly where the finish is.

My friend Martin Hyman, possibly the slowest last-lap man to make the Olympic track team (he finished 8th in the 10,000m), once beat the Olympic champion, Abebe Bikila, in the finish of the Sao Paulo road race, because he knew exactly where the finish was and knew that there was a sharp left hand turn less than 200 metres before the finish. As they approached this road junction, with Bikila just in front, Martin moved to the left and took the left-hand bend as fast as he could, while Bikila was still running down the middle of the road. Martin would agree that Bikila was the better runner, but in sport you have to use your head as well as your legs.

Marathon

One could write a separate book about the mental and physical aspects of marathon running. For most people, the nature of the event is entirely different from races of less than twenty miles, because it is really a fuel economy run. It is you against the course rather than you against the other runners.

The most important thing when running a marathon is maintaining your equilibrium – feeling in control while running as fast as you dare. You have to work out beforehand what time you are likely to do (see Chapter 8) and run the first ten miles (16 km) as close to that target as possible.If you are feeling good you can start to speed up slightly after that, but remember the saying: 'twenty miles is halfway'.

The marathon is chess on legs. Nowhere is it more important to think. This starts by selecting which races to run in. You cannot run more than two or three really good marathons in a year, so you must have an overall strategy, maybe over several years, aimed at a particular goal. Some races give you the opportunity to run fast times, others give the chance to experience different weather conditions and other you may run in because you have a chance of doing well in them, maybe even of winning them.

Each marathon must be followed by a recuperation period and it must be preceded by meticulous preparation. Avoiding injury is the marathon runner's big problem, because his training volume is so big.

Northumberland Castles Race 1995. Road racing sharpens tactical ability.

Assuming that you have selected your race and trained properly, you must plan your tapering and your travelling so that you arrive at the race fresh and eager to race. If you are using altitude training you should come down from altitude between 14 and 21 days before your race. An alternative to this is the five-week plan, where you come down , adjust to the change in the first week and then fit in a couple of time trials or races over the next three weeks. This gives you the confidence-boost from racing, which you might have missed if you have been training at altitude for a long time.

The next vital area lies in predicting what pace you can run and what pace the race is likely to be won at. In the big city marathons, normally spring and autumn, this is less of a problem, because the weather is good enough for optimum times and there will be a pacemaker setting a level-paced first half. The warm-weather race, however, is much more of a lottery. You have to weigh up the effects of the heat and humidity to predict the best that you are capable of. In the 1993 World championships, won in very warm humid conditions, the first two finished in around 2 hr 14,, third was 2 hr 15 and fourth 2 hr 17, yet in this field there were twenty sub-2 hr 11 runners. After halfway, Lucketz Swaartboi speeded up, running the 10km in 30 min 20 sec, but he misjudged things badly, fading to 33 minutes for his next 10km. If someone had been able to predict the winning time correctly he could have run the first half in 66.45 and the second half at the same speed and won comfortably. As it was, only the winner, Mark Plaatjes got near to a perfect race, with splits of 66.30 and 67.27.

The three basic tactics remain the same for the marathon, but played out over two hours rather than a few minutes. The front runner has to have a will of iron to go out from the start and very few, if any, championship marathons have been won that way. Rarely, too, does the race come down to a sprint finish, though that is becoming more likely as the standard of world marathon running rises.

The competitor's guide

Most of what has been said in previous chapters applies to runners of all levels, whatever their goals. What I have to say here is only for the serious competitor, the person to whom winning matters.

When you have put in months or even years of training to prepare for a big event, it is stupid to blow your chances through making mistakes, yet it happens too often. It happens most often when the runner has to become part of a team and take his orders from the team manager or coach. The curious thing is that the runner who puts so much thought into his training and his diet in order to get on the team, is usually quite happy to leave the pre-race arrangements to somebody else – and yet this may be the biggest race of his life, a race which could change his whole future. He may be lucky, if the coach and manager are people with international experience, who put the interests of the runners first, but this is not always the case. The manager may be someone who has earned his place through being a good committee man and a good administrator. He may have forgotten what it was like to be a hungry hyped-up competitor. For example, at the end of a long journey most 'normal' people want to have a drink and a meal, but the serious distance runner will always

want to change and run for at least half an hour before doing anything else. If this has not been allowed for in the itinerary, the athlete will not be happy. The coach, of course, ought to know what the athletes want, but even this is not guaranteed. Each coach has his own way of doing things, which may not be your way. You need to stick to the routines which have been tried and tested, so that you go into the race knowing that you have everything you can. The paragraphs which follow are the fruits of my experience as a competitor and a coach.

Air travel

I love flying, and never more so than when we are getting away from the damp cold of an English winter to somewhere sunny and warm where palm trees grow, but I have seldom known a trip which did not involve a lot of hanging about at the airport. The traveller needs to have a really absorbing book, or some good music, and a relaxed, fatalistic attitude towards delays. He should also have some reserve food – banana, orange, chocolate and a large water bottle, because planes and airport lounges are remarkably dehydrating, and you may find yourself in Khartoum or

Caracas, in an airless lounge at 2 am, with no facilities. During flights one should eat sparingly but take plenty of drinks. For clothing a tracksuit over shorts and a light-weight shirt is best, plus a spare sweater in case you get diverted to Reykjavik. Although it is often free and tempting, I don't recommend drinking a bottle of wine at every meal, because you feel even worse when you arrive.

On all journeys it is a good idea to get up, stretch and move about once every hour. This prevents you from getting into some awkward posture which may cause you to stiffen up. On long-haul flights this is impossible, so I try to go into a coma for most of the flight and then stretch and move about in the last hour.

Altitude training

A lot of mystique surrounds altitude train-ing; at least it does in Britain, where there is nowhere high enough to qualify as 'alti-tude'. In countries which have large areas over 5000 feet (1600m) runners move up to altitude and down again with few prob-lems. It is well-known that distance run-ners cannot run as fast at altitude as they can at sea level and it is equally well-known that after a spell of training up in the highlands you will have reached a higher standard of aerobic fitness and will perform better when you race at sea level.

Physiologists continue to discuss the evidence about the benefits and drawbacks of altitude training; meanwhile the world's best distance runners have been using altitude training as a routine part of their training for more than two decades.

If you walk up a high mountain, the air gets progressively thinner; the amount of oxygen, which makes up one-fifth of the air, naturally declines at the same time, and at 6000 feet the air which you breath into your lungs has 12% less oxygen in the same space as compared with sea-level. Normally the blood, as it passes through the lungs, becomes fully saturated with oxygen, but with less oxygen available, not all the red blood cells pick up their full load of oxygen, and so when they get down to the muscles they cannot always supply the muscles with the oxygen they need. It is alright when you are just walk-ing uphill at, say, 6000 feet, because you just have to breathe harder to take in more oxygen per minute, but the faster you run the more difficult it is to take oxygen in fast enough.

The body becomes stressed due to a shortage of oxygen and in response it man-ufactures more red blood cells, increasing the body's ability to capture and transport oxygen. Naturally, when you come down to sea level again, you are equipped with extra oxygen-carrying cells in a situation where there is no shortage of oxygen. Running becomes easier, and many personal bests have been set within one or two days of returning from altitude. After about the third day there is usually a slight dip in per-formance as the body re-adjusts, but after seven to ten days you start feeling really good. The optimum time for racing after return is between 14 and 21 days, but there is also a knock-on effect. After returning you are able to train harder and push yourself to a higher level. This means that the benefits will last for six weeks or more after return.

The basic rules for altitude training

1. Take it easy for the first five days
2. Drink more water
3. Eat more
4. Sleep more
5. Take extra iron before and during the trip

Altitude training will help you perform better at lower altitudes, as the winner of the 1995 London Marathon, Dionicio Ceron, demonstrates.

Taking it easy

If you train too hard before you are acclimatised, you will damage your immune system. This means that you will be far more likely to pick up coughs and colds. This is a common occurrence when people first go to altitude and the result is that they waste several days of their precious time. I would say that for the first two days no continuous running should be at more than 50% effort, the next two 60% and the fifth day at 70-80% effort. A rough guideline for pulse rates would be: below 140, below 150 and below 160 beats per minute. However, people differ considerably in their pulse rates – younger athletes will be higher than normal and older athletes lower. I was running with a group in Kenya recently and as we got to the top of a hill my pulse was 135 while that of a fit 18-year-old was 166. It is best, therefore, to go on 'perceived effort' and to keep that effort low. An experienced athlete can start hard training as early as the fifth day, but in general the sixth or seventh day is early enough.

The training pattern

The training will be related to the event, of course, but for all events there will be a large element of aerobic training, which comes simply from running over hilly terrain at altitudes of 5500-7500 feet (1600-2300m). Running at track racing speeds must be carefully monitored. Even in the first week it is perfectly alright to do 'leg speed' sessions, involving no more than 50m fast at any time, with long recoveries. The body is not being put under any aerobic stress. Similarly, weight training and circuit training can be done, as long as the work rates are not too intense. During the second week one can train well over relatively short distances, 200-400m, but the recovery times should be twice as long as at sea level. One can also train over long distances, 2 miles/3000m and upwards, where the work-rate is not as high, but one has to be careful of the speed-endurance sessions, the repetition half-miles and kilometres, because these are much more stressful at altitude. Sessions such as 6 x 1000m or 5 x 1200m, run at 5000m pace, can be done in the third week. Speeds will generally be 1-2 seconds a lap slower at 6600 feet (2000m) altitude and the recovery time will have to be extended to allow the pulse rate to fall to a 'plateau' level of 110-120 before starting the next.

Drinking more

Because you are breathing harder you will lose far more water from the lungs, so even when the weather is cool you have to take more fluid, and if you are running in the hot dry climate of Kenya or New Mexico you will lose a tremendous amount of moisture in sweat. You should be drinking an extra litre of water per day at least.

Eating more

Apart from the fact that one is doing a lot of training, the altitude does seems to stimulate the metabolic rate. We find that runners have to eat a lot more carbohydrate to prevent themselves from losing too much weight, and the easiest way to do this is by taking high-carbohydrate drinks after each training session. Whatever the diet, there must be plenty of carbohydrate, whether it is in the form of rice, bread, pasta, potatoes, bananas or the Kenyan standby, *ugali*.

Sleeping more

If the altitude camp is somewhere hot, you will have to train in the early morning. This will allow plenty of time for resting during the middle of the day. We find that one needs an extra hour's sleep at night and an hour or so

Even the best athletes would benefit from a period of altitude training.

after lunch. I have known young athletes sleep for an extra three hours after their morning run.

Taking more iron

Because the body is making more red blood cells it needs extra iron, since iron forms part of the haemoglobin molecule. All runners should have their blood checked every six months anyway to check for any signs of anaemia, but it is a good idea to have a blood test a week before going to altitude and another one as soon as you return. Taking iron tablets in the week before you travel and while you are at altitude will ensure that you have all you need to make extra red cells. Some people take Vitamin C tablets as well, since this helps in the uptake of iron, but if your diet has a high Vitamin C content anyway from eating lots of fresh fruit, this may not be necessary.

Other considerations

The benefits of altitude training go further than just increasing the number of red blood cells, but it is very hard to tell whether these are due solely to the altitude effect or whether they are brought about by training in beautiful surroundings and a good climate. There is usually an increase in the amount of growth hormone produced, which means that you recover more quickly from hard training, and there is an improvement in respiratory capacity too. The only drawbacks seem to be that people pick up coughs and colds more easily. This may be due to sudden changes of tempera-

ture, which are quite common in the mountains.

A major factor in altitude camps is the sun. Because the air is thinner, the sunlight is more intense and the danger of sunburn and dehydration is greater. Runners need to take plenty of sun protection – cream, dark glasses, caps – and to be careful about sun bathing in the middle of the day. Hotter climates bring other hazards, too. One has to be very careful about hygiene. This means keeping food refrigerated, boiling water and peeling fruit; it means being fussy about cleanliness, washing your hands before handling food, disinfecting and protecting any cuts or scratches and protecting yourself against insect bites. There is no point in spending a lot of time and money going off to training camps if you are going to get ill while you are there.

Returning from altitude

There have been some spectacular performances by people the day after they have returned from altitude and running on the third day seems to give very good results too, but after that you should not expect to run really well until at least the eighth day. This means that you can put in a hard session or a time trial immediately after returning, and then carry on with regular running for the rest of the week, without doing anything really hard. From the eighth day onwards you can go back into full training, and I recommend that you aim to reach a peak somewhere between the fifteenth and twenty-first day.

169

Hot climates

When you run, your muscles generate a lot of heat. This causes the blood temperature to rise, and so, in an attempt to keep the body temperature constant, more blood flows to the skin, where heat is lost to the air. At the same time your sweat glands release sweat which evaporates, thus cooling the skin. However, if the air temperature is high and the air is humid, not much heat is lost and not much sweat evaporates. Your blood temperature goes up and you feel uncomfortably hot. You tend to slow your pace, to avoid producing more heat. Your heart rate goes up because blood has to be pumped to the skin as well as the working muscles, and you sweat more. You could lose two litres of sweat in an hour and this would dehydrate you quite seriously if you could not get any drinks. As you become more dehydrated, it is more difficult for the heart to move the blood round the body. In extreme cases

Heat has to be taken seriously.

people collapse Deaths through heat exhaustion in races are rare, but they have happened. Fortunately, there is no reason why this should happen to you, provided you follow some basic principles.

When preparing for a major race in hot weather, you should give yourself at least ten days and preferably two weeks to acclimatise. During that time you should check your body weight daily. It will fall at first, then rise slightly and stabilize at 1-2kg (2-4lb) below your cold-weather norm. In the first two or three days you should just run for half an hour in the morning and the evening, but as you become adjusted, you should try to run every day at the time of your race, so that your body and your mind know what to expect.

In any race over 3km, heat will affect the winning time, though international-class runners are usually affected less than ordinary mortals. Above 15 degrees Celsius the times are going to be slower. A rise of five degrees would slow a top-class runner by 15 seconds over 10 kilometres and by over a minute in a marathon. If a marathon was run at 25 degrees, the top-class runner would probably be 2-3 minutes slower than his best and the three-hour runner 5 minutes slower. If the humidity was really high, 85% or more, the effect would be double this – 5 minutes for the top-class runner, even when acclimatised, 10 minutes for the acclimatised three-hour man and perhaps 20 minutes for the unacclimatised three-hour runner. This obviously affects your decision about the right pace to run in the first half of a long race. The guidelines to follow are:

1. Keep yourself properly hydrated in the last two days before the race. If you drink too much you will find yourself peeing more and your urine will be very pale. If you are dehydrated you will produce less urine and it will be dark yellow.
2. Drink at least 250 ml (half a pint) of water five minutes before the start.
3. Wear loose, light-coloured clothing.
4. Pour water over your head and tie a wet handkerchief round your neck. The evaporation will keep your head cool.
5. Drink every fifteen minutes during the race, trying to take in quarter of a pint

(100ml) at each drink station. This means sipping the drink slowly while you are on the run.
6. Use sponges to keep your head wet.
7. Use whatever shade is provided on the course, i.e., run on the shady side of the street.
8. After the race, keep drinking until you start passing water normally.

If you are running a marathon, the drink should contain glucose or some other carbohydrate (see Carbo-loading), but in shorter events, an isotonic drink or plain water is better.

Cold weather

When it gets cold, our fingers and our ears and noses go red at first, because the body is trying to keep them warm, but as they get colder they go white or even blue, because the body reduces the circulation in the extremities to maintain the core temperature. One wants to avoid over-heating in races, but wearing so little clothing that one is blue with cold is not a good idea either. The extreme cold may cause some blood to be diverted away from your muscles to keep your head warm, and in any case the pain and numbness caused by the

Warm clothing is essential for running in cold climates.

cold may affect your will-power and your judgement. In moderately cold weather (from 5 degrees to 0 degrees C) I suggest wearing a woolly hat, gloves and a long-sleeved T-shirt. In a marathon you can discard the hat and gloves as you go along. In the l994 London Marathon, where it was very cold before the start, I kept myself covered up with a dustbin liner until the gun went. I kept my hat on for the first six miles and kept my gloves on for over twenty miles. Another way of doing it, where you have an early morning start with a big rise in temperature through the morning, is to wear an extra T-shirt at the start and discard it after the first part of the race.

If you are running in sub-zero temperatures – and with a wind-chill factor it may be as low as minus 20 degrees – you will need tights and a long-sleeved T-shirt under your normal running singlet and shorts, as well as the gloves and hat. Some people prefer to cover their arms and legs with a layer of oil, which is anti-social but effective. What you should do is warm-up thoroughly before the race and keep your tracksuit on for as long as possible before the start. Ignore the 'macho' characters who wear nothing but singlets and expose hairy chests – your object is to minimize the effects of the weather and run as efficiently as possible.

'If you can cope with triumph and disaster. . . '

Major competition

The runner who has competed only in local road races or club leagues must be prepared for a shock when he or she first attends a big meeting, such as the English Schools or the AAA Championships. Some are so terrified that they just want to run away and hide, like the Very Small Beetle in the Christopher Robin books. The combination of a strange place, large numbers of strange faces and, particularly, the impersonality of it all, makes the big meeting very daunting and the athlete who started running because it was fun may well think: 'I'm not enjoying this. I wish I was somewhere else.'

It is simply a matter of familiarity. You learn your way around the place, you get to know the other competitors and the officials get to know you; but for the first few of these big events the runner really needs a coach, a parent or a mentor who can provide reassurance and smooth over the difficulties.

For this reason, it is good for athletes to broaden their knowledge and their experience while they are young. The experience of travelling to a different country, sleeping in a strange bed and eating different food can be very stressful, but if the runner belongs to an enlightened club which organizes overseas trips, he will soon learn to adjust.

Perhaps the most trying time of all is the day of the race, when you may have to wait for eight hours or more. You are told not to worry about the race, but you can't stop thinking about it. You have to occupy your time, but you are afraid of tiring yourself out.

There is no easy way around this, but the best approach is to try to structure the time, so that you feel that you are in charge of things and that everything is designed to bring you to the start line in the best possible shape.

Let us say that you are due to race at 5.00 pm, and the stadium is twenty minutes drive from where you are staying. If possible, avoid going to the stadium until you really have to. The ideal plan would be:

8.00 am. Get up, go for a twenty-minute jog in the park, stretch, shower and change.

9.00-10.00 am. Leisurely breakfast, read the papers, tidy up.

10.15 am-12.15 pm. Programme yourself something to do, like a walk round the shops, some studying, even watching a video.

12.15 pm. Go carefully through all the gear you will need for the race and also pack anything else you may need after the race.

12.45-1.30 pm. Lunch. Have a thorough talk with your coach, team manager or team-mate about your plans for the race, so that you have made conscious decisions about the way you are going to run it.

1.45-2.45 pm. Lie down with a book, or just have a nap.

2.45 pm. Check over your bag once more, making sure that you have your number on your vest and that you haven't forgotten your shorts or your racing shoes.

3.00-3.30 pm. Travel to stadium. Spend time checking on the arrangements for reporting in before the race. Find out if the meeting is running to time. Races never start before the scheduled time, but they often start late, and if the meeting is running forty-five minutes behind schedule, adjust your warm-up time. Occasionally they may fool you by cancelling an event and calling for your race only fifteen minutes late, so you have to be in a state of 'amber alert' – partially warmed up with a ten-minute jog – and keeping a close eye on things. If your race is called up suddenly, you will still have time for five minutes striding, two or three minutes stretching and a few more minutes of jogging about. Remember that Ron Hill won one of the greatest marathon races ever with an six-minute warm-up!

The keys to a successful performance lie in the training before the race, the planning of the day before the race and, above all, in a determination that can rise above petty inconveniences. The great competitor knows that he has to keep one part of his mind firmly fixed on the race itself, and this will remain undisturbed by last-minute upsets.

Major games

The climax of an international running career is representing your country in a major Games meeting such as the European or World Championships or the Olympic Games. Once again, the competitor must avoid being overwhelmed by the scale of the affair. He or she must make strenuous efforts to preserve the continuity of the preparation for his particular event. The planning for the last few days of training must come first, because you won't

enjoy the meeting unless you feel that you have done all that you could. Once that is in place, you can think about enjoying the peripheral benefits – seeing a new city, making new friends and supporting your team-mates.

The central matters to get right are those of acclimatisation and adjustment to time zones. Since you will only compete at this level a few times in your life, it is essential to give yourself enough time. If the travelling distance is small with little time change, you need to arrive three days before your event to get settled in. If you have a major climatic or time zone change, you will need a week to ten days in the new conditions. Because life in the Games village can be stressful in itself, it is often a good idea to have an alternative place to stay close by, so that you can get on with your preparation in peace, whilst being close enough to be in touch with the management. If possible, it is a good idea to have some sort of reconnaissance or familiarisation visit a few months beforehand, finding out the best places to train.

This may sound a little fussy, but I go along with Tim Noakes and Bruce Fordyce, 'minute attention to detail, to the point of paranoia'. That's the kind of athlete I like.

Enjoy the Games – they are a high-point of your life – but make sure the race goes well.

Chapter 15

The runner's philosophy

'What's it all about, Alfie?' went the words of a famous song in the sixties. It's a popular phrase. We hear that rugby is all about commitment, that golf is all about accuracy round the greens. We understand what is meant, even though it is wrongly expressed. What they mean is 'commitment is the most important thing', or 'the thing which I emphasize most'. The questions I am attempting to answer are: 'What is the significance of running in our lives?, 'Does running matter at all?, 'Does it matter whether I win or lose?' and 'Does it matter if I drop out?'.

These are questions which we have all asked ourselves; certainly I have pondered them often over the last forty years, on those long runs when I have had no company except my thoughts.

We all have to make choices and running is one of the things we have chosen. The fourteen-year-old can be an actor, a mathematician, a footballer, a musician, a writer and a scientist all in the same day, but sooner or later our options become restricted. Running is a part of your life, maybe an important part, but it is only one of the roles which you play and it inevitably interacts with the others. We are from time to time employees and employers, children and parents, voters,

commuters and do-it-yourself merchants. Many of these roles, however, are forced upon us. We *choose* to become runners or musicians and therefore these activities define our personalities. It is by our success in these chosen fields that we judge ourselves, even though others may look at us from a different aspect.

I can't remember when I didn't run. It is something which our family has always done. At school, where I was very small for my age, I soon discovered that I could beat most people over long distances. In the Army I discovered that being good at running helped me to avoid unpleasant duties. At Southampton University I discovered, more importantly, that running brought me into a group of friends. These friends shared my values. We trained together for a common purpose and although there was a good deal of internal rivalry there was tremendous satisfaction in becoming UAU champions. This led naturally to my joining the best local athletic club, Portsmouth AC, which gave me a regular framework of competition.

All this time I was studying for my degree. I had no father; I depended completely on my student grant for survival and I knew that I had to get a good degree to get a good job, but the dream of becoming a great runner dominated my

English National Cross-Country Championships. These runners have been looking forward to this race for months!

the road and over the country and on one big occasion, the European Championships 5000 metres, I got everything right, won the race and was able to stand on top of the podium and watch the Union Jack climbing into the night sky.

thoughts more and more. Turning out a drawer the other day I came across one of my university files. It had 5000 metre lap times scribbled all down the margins. Luckily the structure of student life enables one to do both things at once, and within a few weeks of getting my degree I found myself winning the AAA Championships at White City – I had been last the year before – and qualifying for the British team to meet the Soviet Union in Moscow. Such experiences etch themselves deeply into the memory. The next few years of running for Britain all over the world were the most exhilarating of my running career. Those years of youth and high ambition had an excitement about them which can never be repeated. In sport you meet what Kipling called 'those two impostors' – triumph and disaster – in rapid succession and you learn a lot from them. I never achieved my ultimate dream of winning the Olympic title – very few do – but I did win international races on the track, on

Since those days I have been involved with running at both ends of the spectrum, as a secondary school teacher coaching boys and girls of all abilities, and as a coach for *Runner's World* magazine, giving advice to adult runners, writing marathon schedules and occasionally competing myself in veteran events. This has given me a perspective on the sport which I never had as an international. It has shown me that the answers to those big questions depend very much on what kind of a runner you are.

The beginner

You have taken up running partly to get fit and partly to find out what it is that people get so hooked on. At first, running is just something which is added on to the other parts of your life. You are not trying to win anything and the only commitment you have made is to yourself. If you pack up after a short time you won't have lost anything – or won't you? You will never know what you have lost. You will never get that feeling of self-mastery, of being in control of your body and being in control of your life which comes from real physical fitness. It is like failing to give up smoking, and represents a failure of will and a loss of self-respect. Give yourself three months to see if it works – that will take you a long way in the First Steps Programme (see Chapter 2) – and if you find after that time that you are not suited to running, physically or temperamentally, then you can try some other form of exercise, but you will not have failed.

The fitness runner

You have been running, on and off, for a couple of years or more. You find that running does you good, and when you are fit you enjoy running, but when life gets hectic and you haven't got time, you lose fitness and then it is a struggle to get going again. Like the beginner, your commitment is only to yourself, so you are the only loser if you quit, but if you know that it does you good and makes you feel good, you have to arrange life so that there *is* time to run. Once it becomes a regular part of your life, it won't be a struggle to get out. The best way of ensuring this is to join a group. Running with other people, sharing experiences and forging common goals makes so much difference. You don't have to make excuses for being a runner. You can talk about your ambitions without

feeling that you are boring anybody. If you get ambitions to run a marathon or to break forty minutes for 10 kilometres, they will be nurtured and encouraged, not ignored or ridiculed. Self-respect is the most valuable thing that we get from running and the respect of others makes a lot of difference.

When it comes to such things as 'Does it matter if I drop out?' or 'Does it matter if I don't run for two months?', you will have your answers when you have clearly defined your goals in your own mind. If you have set goals for the year, say, 'Running twenty miles a week', or 'Breaking the hour for ten miles', then you can build into your year certain times when you are going to be running seriously and certain times when you are taking it easy.

For example, say that you have been running your twenty miles a week for three months and you are feeling very good on it, but you have a work assignment coming up which is going to involve eight weeks of working and travelling in different places. What you say to yourself is: 'I am much fitter than most people because of my running. If I can get out two or three times a week for half an hour, I am going to retain most of that fitness.'

If you have set yourself a time goal, or set a certain race as your goal, then you must act as your own coach. Set yourself a plan and keep a record of what you do alongside the plan. At the end of the schedule you can reward yourself in some way – but you will probably find that achieving your goal is its own reward.

Chapter
15

Eamonn Martin, London Marathon winner of 1993, almost twenty years after his first National Schools' title.

The club runner

You are a regular runner, training at least four times a week. You go training with the club every week and you often race with them on a weekend. You take the trouble to buy the right shoes and wear the right gear. You are always in the first third of the field but you very seldom win anything. On a good day you can make the top twenty in a road race and maybe pick up an award in your age group. You are a valued member of the club team, someone who can be counted on to do his best. On the other hand, you are not getting any

younger and you are unlikely to set any more personal records. Would it matter if you just faded out of the scene?

We come down to self-respect again. Once you have been a serious runner, even at club level, you will always appreciate the need to keep fit. You can decide to reduce your involvement, to compete only at certain times of the year, or to train at a lower level, but if you think back and recognize what running has given you over the years you will know that it is something which you need to keep in your life as you get older.

The committed runner

You may be any age from late teens to mid-thirties. What defines you is your ambition to improve as a runner, improving either in the speed at which you can run or the distance which you can handle, or both. You have a job, but success in your running means at least as much to you as success in your career, for the time being. You have a coach or a mentor, with whom you talk over your training and racing plans. The committed runner is an obsessional type. He has a dream. He is unwilling to compromise in the pursuit of that dream, and because of his obsession he is likely to be unreasonable. Temporary difficulties loom up as major obstacles. Sometimes, each training session becomes a race and each race acquires overwhelming importance. This person can reach the heights but he can also have some terrible lows. I have known people of the highest ability quit the sport because their achievements did not match up to their ideals. Whereas the person of moderate ability might be happy to finish in the top ten in a championship race, the talented runner considers anything outside the first three to be a disaster.

It is this kind of person who is most in need of a balanced running philosophy. He must learn to accept that improvement will not always be in a steady upward curve. He must realize that injuries will occur if he trains too hard, but that injuries are only temporary setbacks, not the end of a career. He must enjoy his minor successes and be realistic in his yearly goals.

For this kind of person, running is a central part of their personality. Dropping out of a race is regarded as a personality failure – whereas it may simply be a bad cold.

To answer those questions at the beginning of the chapter – running is a significant part of your life at this stage, because you have chosen to make it so. Later you may develop into another phase of your life where it is quite unimportant. In the meantime, you will get the most out of your running if you set your standards high. By maintaining your self-discipline and meeting your challenges you will become not only a better runner but also a better person.

The harder you train and the more serious you become about your running, the greater the dangers of it taking over your life completely. You can take the sport seriously, but you should never take yourself too

seriously. Dropping out of a race may matter to you, but no one else will give a damn.

The more solitary you are, the harder it is to keep yourself balanced. The runner needs to have someone around – coach, partner, parent or friend – to keep his feet on the ground. When he goes to the national championships he should have two pieces of paper in his pockets. One piece says: 'This race is a test of your strength, an examination of your philosophy, a judgement on your way of life'. The other piece of paper says: 'It's only a race'.

The professional runner

The committed runner may evolve into the professional runner if he has the talent and is willing to take the gamble. As Nick Rose once said: 'It's better than wrapping chocolates' (Nick left school at sixteen and got his first job in the Fry's chocolate factory, before he got a track scholarship in the USA). Such a person is bound to take a different attitude to the sport. There will be times when economic common-sense demands that he runs the big-city marathon rather than represent his country in an international. Life is not easier for the full-time runner, whatever the part-time runners may feel. True, he has more time to train, but the need to keep on earning money means that he sometimes has to race when he would rather not. The dangers of injury are far more serious for him than for the amateur, and the likelihood of getting injured is greater because he is running at

Chapter 15

Athlete and Coach. Richard Nerurkar and Bruce Tulloh.

such a high level. The decision about whether to race and how often to race is often made for economic reasons rather than strategic reasons.

At heart, though, he still lives in dreams, as we all do. There must be times in his career when he puts the dream first and the money second, otherwise he will always regret what might have been.

The parting word

We are given one life and we are given certain gifts. It may take us twenty years to find what those gifts are, but if we have any duties at all, the first is to ourselves, to use our gifts properly.

If you think you are a runner, get out and run! And enjoy it! I do.

Loosening and stretching

These should be done when the muscles are warm, i.e., after a warm-up jog and at the end of a run. Hold each stretch for ten seconds, without making it painful.

1. Arm swinging. Six to ten circles forwards and backwards.

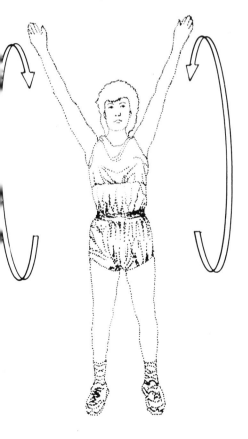

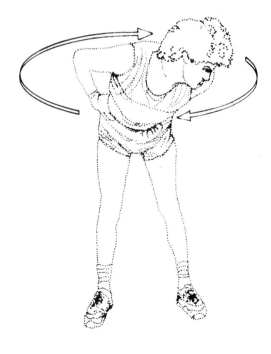

2. Hip rotation. Keep your knees straight, while circling the trunk and rotating the hips, six to ten times each way.

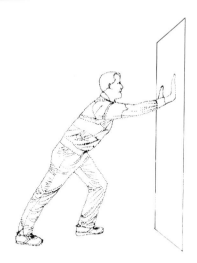

3. Lower leg stretch. Lean forwards steadily, feeling a gentle stretch on the calf muscles and Achilles tendon. Do three with each leg.

5. Hamstrings and gluteal stretch. Keep your back straight, while pulling your knee towards your chest. Can also be done lying down.

4. Quads and ankles stretch. Pull the leg backwards and outwards, stretching the muscles on the front of the thigh. While holding the stretch, rotate the free ankle. Do three with each leg.

6. Side stretch. Lean sideways as far as possible. Do three on each side.

7. Adductor stretch. Legs wide apart and kept straight. Lean the body forwards at the waist, pressing the palms of the hands towards the floor. Hold for 30 secs, relax, repeat 3 more times. This may be done standing or sitting.

8. Groin stretch. Push body downwards and forwards, like a fencer's lunge, keeping your body straight.

Appendix B

Sprint drills

SD1 Skipping

Skipping on alternate legs. As the athlete hops forward on the left foot, the right knee is raised high, then the athlete hops on the right leg, raising the left knee high. The arms should be moved vigorously, to help the knee action. Do five times 30 metres, with a slow 30 metre jog between each.

SD2 High knees

At each stride an exaggerated arm action is used and the knees are brought up as high as possible. The stride length is kept short. Do five times 25 metres, with a slow 30 metre walk-jog after each.

SD3 Bottom kicking

The athlete jogs along, taking very short (50cm) strides. At each stride, the back leg is pulled up behind, as fast as possible. Do five times 30 metres, with a slow 30 metre walk-jog after each.

SD4 Bounding

This is done like a slow-motion sprint, with the athlete driving hard with the arms and pulling the front leg high so as to get the maximum length at each bound. A vigorous drive is needed from the take-off leg, so that the athlete goes high in the air. Do five times 40 metre walk-jog after each.

Appendix C

Weight training

Because you are imposing extra strain on the body, weight training exercises must be done properly. The best thing is to go to a weight training gym and be shown the correct way to perform an exercise. Lifting a heavy weight incorrectly can cause damage

There are dozens of different exercises and many different systems, some of them very elaborate. The six exercises I have given here can be done with simple equipment and are suitable for runners. All except W2 develop leg strength.

For distance runners, I do not advise weight training with anything like the maximum weight you can manage. It is safest to start by using only 50-60% of your maximum – something which you can manage to do ten times in succession.

The advantage of weight training is that it is measurable and can easily be made progressive. Start by doing each exercise eight times, going through the six in the order shown, with only a short break between each, then do another complete set (six exercises, eight times each). Repeat this three or four days later. The following week, try three sets of eight each. When you can manage three sets of ten with each exercise, increase the weight and drop the number back to six or eight.

Weights are best used at a time when you are not competing very seriously. When you reach the racing period, weights can either be cut out completely, or kept in once a week at a reduced level, so that they do not tire you for races.

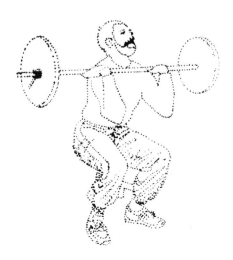

W1 Half-squats
The weight is held at shoulder level. Go up onto your toes, keeping your back straight and lower your body until your thighs are parallel to the ground, then straighten up.

185

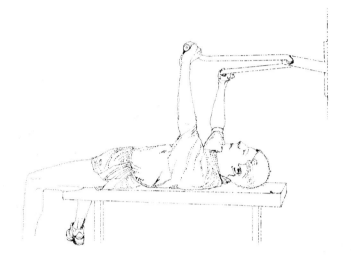

W2 Bench press

Lie on your back on a bench, with the weight held across and just above your chest. Breathe normally and straighten your arms until the elbows are locked, then lower the weight back to just above your chest.

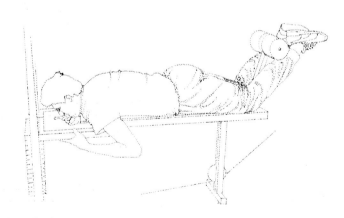

W3 Hamstring curl

Lie on your front, with the weight across the back of your ankle. Pull your feet upwards until your shins are vertical, then lower again.

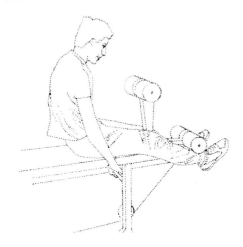

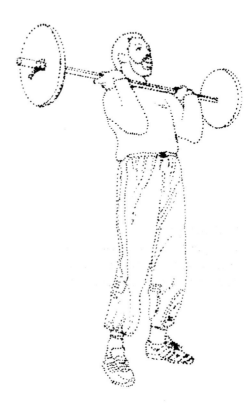

W4 Quadriceps curl
Sit on the end of the bench, with the weight across the front of your foot. Pull your feet forwards, straightening both legs, while keeping the rest of the body immobile.

W5 Power clean
Start in the position shown. Straighten your legs first and when your legs are nearly straight, pull your forearms upwards, so that the weight comes up to your shoulders. As this happens, straighten your legs so that you finish up in position shown. Complete the exercise by letting the bar down to waist level, then, keeping your back straight, lower the weight to the floor.

W6 Heel raises

Get the weight across your shoulders. This
may be on a bar, or it may be a fixed
weight. Your toes should be raised higher
than your heels, as shown. Tighten your
calf muscles and raise yourself forwards
onto your toes, so that your heels come
clear of the ground, then lower them
again.

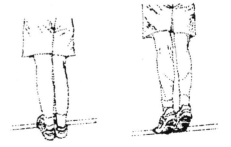

Circuit training

Circuit training is used in a variety of sports to develop and maintain all-round fitness. The number of different exercises and combinations is infinite, but a typical circuit will consist of between eight and ten different exercises, which between them will cover all the main muscle groups.

Although weights may be used, these are mostly light. The emphasis is on doing the exercises fast and moving quickly from one to the next. We thus get an improvement in muscular endurance as well as strength and if the whole set is done fast with short recoveries, we will get a cardiovascular benefit as well. It is usual to have a separate place or 'station' for each exercise, so that you can have as many people working at once as there are stations.

Start by doing 30 secs of each exercise and go round one circuit, moving as quickly as you can between stations. Count how many you manage of each exercise. Give yourself three or four minutes recovery and then go round again, doing the same number of exercises. With a group, it is best to have a set time on each station, but if you are doing them on your own, it is easier to give yourself a fixed number to do.

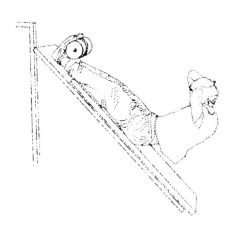

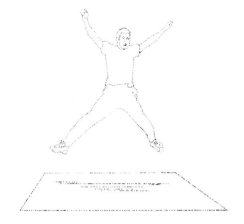

C1 Sit-ups

These may be done as shown, or lying flat on the floor. If you cannot manage them with your arms behind your head, put your hands down by your side, or on your thighs.

C2 Star-jumps

Start in a squatting position, then leap high in the air and comeback to squatting position again.

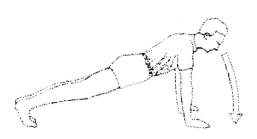

C3 Trunk raises

If you haven't got a machine, you can do a similar exercise just lying flat on a mat and arching your back.

C5 Press-ups

Keep your body straight and lower it until your chest is almost touching the ground.

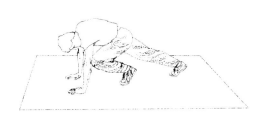

C4 Half-squats

These are best done with a light weight, or holding a dumb-bell in each hand. Stand with feet slightly apart, come up onto your toes, then, keeping your back straight, go down until your thighs are parallel to the ground.

C6 Leg changes

Start in the position shown, then bring the back leg forwards and shoot the front leg back, trying to keep your body rigid.

C7 Calf raises (illustrated as W6 in Appendix C)
Stand on a step or a wooden bar, so that your heels are lower than your toes. Tighten your calf muscles and come up onto your toes, then lower again. This exercise is more effective if you are carrying weights or dumb-bells at shoulder level.

C8 (not illustrated)
Stand with your feet slightly apart, clench your fists and drive your arms backwards and forwards in an exaggerated running action.

Many circuits finish off with two or three minutes skipping or pedalling a static bike, but if you are running regularly, this is not essential.

Index